Parenting a High-Functioning Autistic Toddler

9 Key Strategies to Understanding Autism and Helping Your Little One Build a Healthy Relationship With Family and Peers

Obie Ighodalo-Eromosele

been derived from various sources. Please consult a licensed professional before attempting any techniques outlined in this book.

By reading this document, the reader agrees that under no circumstances is the author responsible for any losses, direct or indirect, that are incurred as a result of the use of the information contained within this document, including, but not limited to, errors, omissions, or inaccuracies.

Table of Contents

Trigger Warning: This book may contain anecdotes and descriptions regarding spectrum disorders, including the problems parents and toddlers face. These scenarios may be disturbing or triggering for some readers.

Introduction

What would happen if the autism gene was eliminated from the gene pool? You would have a bunch of people standing around in a cave, chatting and socializing and not getting anything done. –Dr. Temple Grandin

Being a parent of a neurodivergent child is a never-ending job. Becoming a parent is a huge responsibility on its own. You are the sole provider and caregiver for a whole human being until they become independent and can take care of themselves. That's a huge task for anyone, and no one really knows what the right way is to bring up a child these days, because everyone is just doing their best.

Having a toddler who is neurodivergent comes with an array of unique challenges that are hard to imagine during those nine months of anticipation. Nothing can truly prepare you to be a parent of a toddler who needs more than most, may not hit the milestones, or has different needs than neurotypical toddlers. It's all so new and all so scary when you are first faced with the reality of life as the parent of a special-needs toddler.

Here you are, in the depths of it, trying to figure out what to do and how to do it. This parenting thing can be so overwhelming. Whether it's making sure your child has their comfort plushie with them at all times, or their noise-canceling headphones on in public places, or cutting out the tags from all their clothes; it's way more than the average parent considers. That feeling of regret, shame, and fear when you know your child is on the verge of a meltdown in public, or when you can't figure out why your child is stimming, or when you feel like you're doing something that's causing them anxiety.

When these thoughts, feelings, and situations keep occurring you can't help but question whether you are a good parent or not. You probably have days when you feel like you really don't know what you are doing. Nothing can compare to the days when society judges you and your child blindly without considering that they are autistic or that you are simply doing your best in that moment. Helplessness is an emotion that plagues you as the parent of a neurodivergent child, but it doesn't have to always be like this.

You have ways to help yourself and your child. This book can be one of the tools you need to gain the skills you may currently lack. You may need more information about your child's diagnosis or their possible symptoms that need managing. This is a great first step to educating yourself and helping your toddler develop some great coping mechanisms. This book provides nine ways you can work with your autistic toddler and help them gain some valuable skills. There will also be some tips you can include in your daily routine to make things more manageable for everyone.

The information in this book was gathered over a long period of time, consulting a large variety of sources and analyzing research across the world regarding high-functioning autistic toddlers. Research and consideration of your individual needs were taken into account to produce an objective and helpful book. These details have been proven to provide the best results, since solutions, strategies, and practical answers are of the highest priority. By the end, you should have the skills to address and deal with your toddler's needs while understanding their condition. You will be able to help your toddler communicate effectively and gain significant social skills, thus helping them gain some independence, confidence, and coping mechanisms for a more fulfilling future.

The author is a health care professional who has had extensive experience with all types of toddlers. She often encountered toddlers who weren't "typical" and who left her wondering how she could help them. Soon she found herself working with toddlers who had different disabilities, and she developed wonderful empathy for these toddlers and their families. She hopes to help parents find ways to connect and become more involved in the direct care of their toddlers. Through acknowledging, accepting, and getting involved, she hopes parents have a more fulfilling relationship with their autistic toddlers.

This culmination of research, writing, and experience has led to this incredibly curated piece of work. Twelve chapters of understanding to be found, tips to be used, and activities to be done with your toddler. You are about to become enlightened and find ways to help your toddler without leaving the comfort of your own home. Your family's journey is just beginning.

Chapter 1: High-Functioning Autism (HFA) Spectrum Disorder

Autism spectrum disorder (ASD) is a neurological and developmental disorder that affects how people interact with others, communicate, learn, and behave. Although autism can be diagnosed at any age, it is classified as a "developmental disorder" because symptoms typically appear in the first two years of life.

According to the Centers for Disease Control (2018), one in every 44 American toddlers has autism. Autism manifests itself in a variety of ways, the majority of which are caused by a combination of inherited and environmental factors. Autism spectrum disorder patients have a wide range of learning, reasoning, and problem-solving abilities, ranging from extremely skilled to severely disabled.

Some autistic people may require a great deal of assistance in their daily lives. Others may require less assistance and, in some cases, be able to live independently. Autism can be caused by a variety of conditions, and it frequently coexists with sensory sensitivity issues as well as medical conditions such as gastrointestinal issues, seizures, or sleep difficulties.

Autism symptoms typically appear around the age of 2 or 3; additional developmental problems may also be present. According to the National Institute of Neurological Disorders and Stroke (2022), early intervention helps autistic people achieve their goals later in life. The American Psychiatric Association coined the term "autism spectrum disorder" in 2013 after combining four distinct autism diagnoses.

Individuals who interact with people who have ASD believe that someone can be high-functioning on the spectrum of any condition. Even social media has evolved into a platform for accurate portrayals of how the majority of autistic people, particularly teenagers and young toddlers, live in our culture and communities.

What Is High-Functioning Autism?

It can be difficult to know how to raise a child with HFA, given the difficulties that people on the autism spectrum already face. When you can't get private care, the information you get as a parent of a toddler with autism is all you have. This is why it is critical to become acquainted with the nuances of HFA toddlers' characteristics. Knowing your toddler's spectrum disorder allows you to develop specialized skills and tactics to help them grow into a better version of themselves.

Before the age of three, early speech and language development has been shown to be severely delayed. This has been used as the primary indicator of high-functioning autism by psychologists. The first of three types of autism, level one, is known as "high-functioning." This demonstrates a person's ability to speak, read, write, and manage daily responsibilities such as dressing and eating. Regardless of the symptoms, their behavior has no discernible impact on their academic, professional, or interpersonal relationships.

Children with "high-functioning autism" are typically brilliant, social, resourceful, and talkative, despite having fewer visible symptoms of the disorder. For the purposes of this text and comprehension, we'll refer to this type of autism as "high-functioning." It has been questioned whether describing people as "high-functioning" or "low-functioning" in the same sentence is appropriate.

The first step is to understand HFA and how it affects your toddler. Autism spectrum disorder includes high-functioning autism. Each autistic child is unique, and their symptoms can range from mild to severe. The term "high-functioning autism" is relatively new. However, it is not a recognized medical diagnosis, and many people are still debating whether it can be used to define a subset of autism, specifically those who can talk, read, write, and manage basic life skills without much assistance. They are capable of surviving on their own.

This is not to say that toddlers with high-functioning autism do not face problems or obstacles. Because each child is unique, it is impossible to generalize a single experience and apply it to every family or child. It is critical to be aware of how your toddler may interact, react, and express themselves in order to avoid comparing them to texts or articles.

In fact, symptoms that make doing routine activities complex or difficult are common in toddlers with high-functioning autism. One of the most difficult issues they face is social interaction with others. Given the importance of social connections in reaching developmental milestones, this may be cause for concern. They may also struggle with motor skills considered essential for high-functioning toddlers, such as writing. These are undoubtedly assumptions that may make it difficult for your toddler to engage and learn as intended.

Some toddlers with high-functioning autism may have co-occurring conditions such as anxiety, attention deficit hyperactivity disorder (ADHD), or depression. These conditions are not always caused by autism; rather, it is more likely that they are inherited or that stressful situations have led to disordered behavior as a coping mechanism.

Common Symptoms of High-Functioning Autism

It is important to be able to identify and understand the symptoms of someone who has high-functioning autism. High-functioning autism (HFA) is a form of autism that is characterized by milder symptoms and a higher IQ. These are some general symptoms that may occur; they may develop after some time or may be presenting themselves in your toddler right now.

- **Language peculiarities:** People with HFA often have difficulty with social interactions and may be seen as "odd" or "eccentric." This could be because their responses are blunt or they may not even acknowledge what someone else may be saying. Kids with HFA typically have a better grasp of language than kids with low-functioning autism (LFA). A child may have HFA if they consistently use unusual wording and phrasing in conjunction with a limited range of interests.

- **Social problems:** They may have trouble reading nonverbal cues such as body language or facial expressions. They struggle with identifying tone and pitch as well as determining overall how someone else may be feeling. They may also have trouble starting or maintaining conversations. They may not be able to tell that someone wants to talk to them. So they may have trouble understanding the dynamics of a conversation.

- **Little or no attention to caregivers:** Children with High-Functioning Autism have difficulty maintaining eye contact with their parent or another adult. They may not interact with caregivers in the same way that other toddlers do. If a child fails to turn to the caregiver for a shared interest, they may lack this social skill.

- **Sensory difficulties:** Many HFA toddlers experience sensory issues. These could appear in one or all of them (sight, sound, smell, touch, or taste). The child would typically perceive common feelings as fairly powerful or underreact to a sense. The difficulty in this field will be determining whether a child's response to a stimulus is a sensory reaction or a learned habit motivated primarily by stiffness and fear.

- **Repetitiveness:** People with HFA may also exhibit repetitive behaviors such as hand-flapping, spinning in circles, or repetition of words or phrases. Some people with HFA also have interests that are unusual or intense such as trains, numbers, or animals, or preoccupation with a specific topic or activity, which can be beneficial or detrimental. Excellence that develops as a result of increased interest in a particular topic can be extremely beneficial. Finding toddlers with similar interests can also promote social interaction and activities.

Additionally, people with HFA often have trouble with executive functioning skills. This can include planning and organization. Imaginative play as well as sustained attention are affected by HFA. They may also have difficulty with motor skills.

Differences Between High-Functioning Autism and Asperger's Syndrome

Asperger's syndrome, formerly known as HFA, has been designated an autism spectrum disorder by the American Psychiatric Association. Despite the fact that high-functioning ASD is no longer recognized as a diagnosis, some people continue to self-identify as having it.

People with Asperger's syndrome shared several symptoms with autistic people, but they did not experience delays in:

- verbal communication

- cognitive growth

- age-appropriate self-help skill development

- the evolution of receptive behavior

- growing interest in their surroundings

Compared to autistic people, their symptoms were frequently less severe and less likely to interfere with their daily lives. They might have even been regarded as "high-functioning."

The DSM-5 (Diagnostic and Statistical Manual of Mental Disorders) removed Asperger's syndrome and a few other neurodevelopmental disorders, but HFA has never received a formal clinical diagnosis. People who exhibit repetitive or restricting behavior or who struggle with social interaction and communication would now be classified as having a spectrum disorder. This is true regardless of how much assistance they might require. Then, according to their ability to function, there would be other classifications assigned.

These additional characteristics differentiate those with HFA from those with Asperger's syndrome:

- Lower capacity for verbal reasoning: An Asperger's diagnosis requires no significant impairments in language.

- Greater performance IQ and improved visual/spatial skills: HFA is categorized by an IQ of 70 and higher and they can understand certain spatial tasks.

- Less erratic movement (such as clumsiness): HFA and Asperger's both present with fine motor difficulties, however HFA is categorized by a higher severity.

- Issues with independence: There is potential for independence when their impairments are nurtured and developed during childhood. Those with Asperger's are more likely to lead independent lives with little assistance.

- Interest and curiosity about a wide range of topics compared to Asperger's syndrome, which is categorized by specific topics of fixation.

- Lack the capacity for empathy for others and struggle with identifying or learning about human emotion.

- Significantly lower (4:1) male to female ratio, while Asperger's is significantly higher in males.

Asperger's syndrome and HFA are both characterized by difficulties with social interaction and communication. Even though they share some characteristics, there are several key differences. Individuals with HFA, for example, frequently have more severe symptoms than those with Asperger's syndrome, as well as more difficulty with social interaction and communication.

There is no recognized definition of HFA in the medical field. When people use this phrase, they probably mean something that resembles level 1 ASD. People with HFA may also have more difficulty with communication, both verbal and nonverbal.

There are 3 levels to ASD:

- **Level 1:** These individuals might experience symptoms that don't significantly affect their relationships, careers, or academic endeavors. When people talk about HFA or Asperger's syndrome, they typically mean this.

- **Level 2:** Individuals in this level regularly need some outside assistance. Speech therapy and social skills instruction are two examples of outside support.

- **Level 3:** People at this level consistently need a lot of outside assistance. Full-time aides or intensive therapy may be used as forms of support in some circumstances.

When you understand that there are distinct differences, you will be able to help your toddler in specific ways that cater to their unique needs.

Compared to those with Asperger's syndrome, people with HFA frequently engage in more repetitive behaviors. Although those with Asperger's syndrome may also have trouble communicating and interacting with others, their symptoms are typically milder than those of people with HFA. Additionally, they might interpret jokes or sarcasm literally and have trouble understanding humor. They might also find it difficult to maintain conversations or make friends. Both Asperger's syndrome and HFA have no known cures, but there are treatments that can lessen symptoms.

Controversy Surrounding the Term "High-Functioning Autism"

The lack of accuracy in the term "high-functioning" is the primary reason it is divisive in the autism community. The term "high-functioning autism" is typically used to describe an autistic person who does not suffer from an intellectual disability. However, studies, including one from 2019, have shown that there is only a weak relationship between IQ and adaptive behaviors, such as eating, dressing, tying shoes, and so on (Howard, 2021).

Therefore, defining "high-functioning" involves more than just measuring intelligence. In other words, it would be inaccurate to categorize an autistic person as either high- or low-functioning given the wide range of functioning categories in society, including

- ability to communicate

- social conscience

- processing information

- sensory analysis

- motor capabilities

These categories affect all autistic people differently. An autistic person with a high IQ, for instance, would generally be categorized as "high-functioning" yet could still score low in all social and communication categories.

People believe that the term completely ignores the challenges these people face on a daily basis. The worry is that people who are classified as "high-functioning" won't have access to the treatment and services they require. Without a more comprehensive assessment, an autistic person who would benefit from therapy and other services might not be eligible for funding because the areas where they experience difficulties have been ignored or overlooked.

Because it implies a hierarchy among people with autism spectrum disorders, the term is divisive. The term "high-functioning autism," according to some, is ableist because it implies that people who do not exhibit high functioning are somehow less capable. Others counter that the phrase is merely descriptive and not meant to be disparaging.

Some claim that the term "high-functioning autism" is inaccurate because it suggests that all autistic people have high functioning. Others contend that the term can be helpful in determining who might require more support and ensuring that these people receive the proper level of care. Ultimately, how each autistic person uses and interprets the term will determine whether or not it is controversial.

It is quite evident that the expectations of the term are where the controversy lies. As a parent, referring to your toddler as "high-functioning" means that you have a direct responsibility to understand the meaning of the term as well as explain the possible misunderstandings that come along with the terminology. It also means that you cannot place unnecessary expectations or hopes on your toddler's coping skills or abilities just because they exhibit certain "high-functioning" traits. They may succeed at many things but still struggle with other things—and that is okay, because your toddler is not like any other child and their experience is unique.

Chapter 2: Myths About High-Functioning Autism

It's possible that you've heard some inaccurate information about HFA. There are many myths and misconceptions about autism and those who have it. To make sure that autistic people receive the support, assistance, and understanding they both need and deserve, it's crucial that we dispel these myths about autism because they can be upsetting, harmful, stigmatizing, or just plain misleading.

Common Myths About High-Functioning Autism

We now know a great deal more about autism than ever before because of rising awareness, research, and more inclusive and thorough definitions of what autism is. But there is still a great deal we don't understand. The most important thing is to make sure that we and those around us are properly informed about the facts and myths surrounding autism.

Myth 1: Autism Is a Mental Disorder

Autism is not a mental disorder. It is a neurodevelopmental disorder that affects how a person communicates and interacts with others. While people with autism may have some challenges with social interaction and communication, they are just as capable of leading happy and successful lives as anyone else.

With the right support and a suitable environment, many autistic people are very capable and independent. Around 1 in 4 autistic people speak few or no words, but they can find other ways to communicate. Some autistic people take longer to process information, but it doesn't mean they don't understand. Autistic people also have some advantages over those without autism. For example, strong attention to detail and a special ability for seeing patterns in data can bring many advantages.

Myth 2: People With Autism Always Have Savant Abilities

Another pervasive misconception among the myths about autism—perpetuated by media, such as movies like *Rain Man* and TV shows *The Big Bang Theory* and *The Good Doctor*—is that all autistic people have savant skills. A savant skill, caused by savant syndrome, is a very rare condition in which someone exhibits extraordinary and exceptional mental abilities. This might be related to memory, art, music, or rapid calculation.

Not every autistic person will go on to become the next Albert Einstein. It is not yet conclusive as to why approximately 28% of autistic people have exceptional abilities. Some autistic people have savant abilities, which are extraordinary abilities such as a great memory or mathematical prowess. Savant abilities are only found in a small percentage of autistic adults, and not all savants are autistic.

Myth 3: Autism Can Be Cured

The condition of autism cannot be cured, but it can be managed. Many individuals with autism can lead contented lives with the help of early intervention and ongoing treatment. It is not something that can be grown out of or simply treated with medication and then deemed "normal."

Although everyone with autism experiences it differently, the majority of autistic adults and their families believe that autism is a significant aspect of their lives and is not something they would like to do without. With the aid of research, autistic people will be able to receive the services and support they require in order to live long, fulfilling lives. Autism is a complex condition that affects everyone differently, so it is important to focus on every autistic person's individual needs in order to help them cope in their own way.

Myth 4: People With Autism Are Always Socially Awkward

People with autism can be socially awkward, but not all of them are. Many people with autism are able to form strong social bonds and lead rich social lives. It is a common misconception that people with autism are socially awkward. While some people with autism may struggle with social relationships, this is not the case for everyone. Some people with autism have strong social skills and can easily interact with others, whereas others struggle with social interactions but can still form meaningful relationships with others.

Myth 5: High-Functioning Autism Is Just a Made-Up Diagnosis

Undoubtedly, some autistic individuals are capable of high functioning. People with milder symptoms and those who can function reasonably well in society are affected by this type of autism. It is disliked despite not being inaccurate because of the expectations that "high-functioning" fosters. We can contribute to reducing the conversations surrounding this myth by simply defining what high-functioning means.

Initially, it was widely regarded. However, when people started to notice that the general public was confused that an HFA child still needed assistance, they encountered problems. The assumptions of society are the problem, not the spectrum on which autistic toddlers exist.

Myth 6: People With High-Functioning Autism Are Just Really Smart

Having HFA does not necessarily mean being intelligent. Even though there are many autistic people who are extremely intelligent, not all of them are geniuses. In actuality, just like the general populace, people with autism exhibit a wide range of intelligence levels. People with HFA may have average or above-average intelligence, but intelligence is not a defining characteristic of the condition.

Myth 7: People With High-Functioning Autism Don't Feel Emotions

This is among the most prevalent misconceptions about HFA. It doesn't necessarily mean that when someone doesn't show their emotions, they can't feel them. It simply means that they find it difficult to express them. In actuality, those with HFA may be extremely sensitive to emotions and even feel them more intensely than average. This is due to many reasons, such as hypersensitivity and poor emotional regulation. People with HFA can experience and express emotions, though they may have difficulty understanding and interpreting the emotions of others.

Myth 8: People With High-Functioning Autism Don't Want Friends

Although individuals with HFA may have fewer friends than others, this does not mean that they do not desire them. Many individuals with HFA yearn for close relationships, but struggle to make and maintain friends because of their social challenges. People with HFA, like anyone else, may want and seek out friendships. They may struggle with social interactions and communication, but this does not mean they do not desire connections with others.

It is critical to recognize that autism is a spectrum disorder, which means that it affects each individual differently. Some autistic people have more severe symptoms, while others have fewer. As a result, generalizing about the abilities of all people with autism is incorrect. It is critical to treat everyone with respect and to recognize that everyone is unique, with their own set of strengths and weaknesses.

Chapter 3: Strategies for Parenting Toddlers With High-Functioning Autism

While there is no cure-all for autism, there are many different approaches you can take to help your toddler develop their skills and manage their symptoms. Early intervention is key. The earlier a child receives therapy and support, the better their chances of developing social, communication, and cognitive skills. Seek out therapies such as applied behavior analysis (ABA), speech and language therapy, and occupational therapy to help your toddler develop these skills.

9 Key Strategies for Parenting Toddlers With High-Functioning Autism

It is important to understand what you are getting yourself into. First, you have to understand the basics of each of the nine strategies before you get into the details of learning and practicing these skills and activities. Take a moment to look at the whole picture by going through the following strategies that will be covered over the next few chapters.

Communication

Children with autism frequently speak in ways that other toddlers do not. They could find it challenging to communicate with and be understood by others as a result. Most toddlers begin to pick up on nonverbal signs as babies when they seek their parents' approval. For toddlers with autism, the ability to "tune in" to the thoughts and feelings of others does not develop at the same rate. Due to their frequent lack of social skills, it can be very difficult for kids with HFA to make friends and develop meaningful relationships with others. According to studies, kids who have trouble communicating with others may pick up a variety of vital skills that will make socializing much easier.

Communicating with high-functioning autistic toddlers can be challenging, but it is critical to provide positive feedback and encouragement as the kid learns and grows. Using visual aids, such as pictures or videos, to help the child understand what you are saying; using gestures or sign language to supplement verbal communication; and providing the child with plenty of opportunities to practice their communication skills in a safe and supportive environment are some effective strategies.

Pretend Play

Pretend play allows your toddler to practice social skills in a safe and supervised environment. You will also have the opportunity to teach your toddler how to behave in social situations. Playing pretend with toys, puppets, or everyday items can be done in a variety of ways. The most important aspect is to have fun and be creative! Children with autism play differently than those who do not have the condition. Pretend play can help your toddler with HFA improve their social and communication skills. They usually prefer to perform acts and arrange items rather than pretend to be someone else. With the help of a variety of therapies, toddlers with autism and their families can play together.

According to specialists, high-functioning autistic toddlers may require additional care and supervision in comprehending social conventions and engaging in play with others. They can flourish and acquire crucial skills via play if you provide a caring and nurturing atmosphere for them. It is also critical to be patient and empathetic, particularly with young toddlers. It is critical to establish a regulated and predictable setting while practicing play with high-functioning autistic toddlers. This can make toddlers feel more at ease and safe, allowing them to engage in play more readily. Allowing ample youngsters time for play and exploration is equally critical for their cognitive and social development.

Bonding

Children with autism behave, think, and communicate in ways that their typically developing peers do not. The fact that these toddlers do not interact with their surroundings in the same way that neurotypical toddlers do does not preclude relationships from developing with them. There are several ways to form a strong bond with your toddler. Many parents of autistic toddlers struggle to find hobbies and activities that give their autistic child a sense of accomplishment. If you have a good relationship with your HFA toddler, they will feel more loved and secure. If you have a close relationship with your toddler, you will be better able to understand their needs.

Bonding with your toddler is an important aspect of parenting, regardless of whether your toddler has autism or not. For parents of high-functioning autistic toddlers, bonding can be especially important for building a strong and positive relationship with your toddler. Some strategies for bonding with your toddler may include

- spending one-on-one time with your toddler, such as reading a book together or playing a game

- engaging in activities that your toddler enjoys and is interested in

- showing interest in your toddler's interests and accomplishments

- providing positive reinforcement and support for your toddler's efforts and successes

- communicating openly and honestly with your toddler, listening to their thoughts and feelings, and responding in a supportive and understanding way

It's important to remember that every child is different, and what works for one child may not work for another. It may take some trial and error to find the right bonding strategies for your toddler. It may also be helpful to seek support from a therapist or other professional who can help you develop effective bonding strategies for your toddler.

Socializing

Many autistic toddlers and adults require assistance in learning appropriate social behavior in a variety of social situations. You could sign them up for social skills classes or extracurricular activities. Always be patient and allow your toddler to progress at their own pace. They will gradually develop the skills needed to interact with others in a way that feels natural to them. It may be difficult for toddlers with HFA to interact with others. They must improve their interpersonal communication abilities. Your child's mental health and overall quality of life are dependent on their social skills. The development of social skills can lead to increased community involvement and positive outcomes such as happiness and friendships.

If you are the parent of a high-functioning autistic toddler, you may be looking for ways to help them improve their social skills. This could involve setting up playdates with other toddlers or joining a social skills group. It may also be helpful to model appropriate social behavior and provide positive reinforcement. Working with a therapist who has experience with autism can provide valuable support and guidance.

Using the Senses

Sensory stimulation is extremely beneficial for autistic toddlers. The child's learning process should consider their senses of touch, taste, smell, hearing, and vision. Use your imagination when providing sensory stimulation to your toddler. What your toddler enjoys or seeks should help you decide what to use. Sensory stimulation in learning refers to activities that test the five senses of touch, taste, smell, hearing, and seeing. Sensory stimulation benefits both learning and a child's emotional and social development. Many toddlers with HFA are overly sensitive to specific stimuli. To help them cope with sensory overload, give them fidget toys or noise-canceling headphones.

It is important to provide sensory experiences for high-functioning autistic toddlers in order to help them develop and learn. Sensory activities can help them learn to process and interpret sensory information, and can also provide a calming and enjoyable experience. Some examples of sensory activities for high-functioning autistic toddlers include playing with textured toys, listening to music, and exploring nature. It is also important to provide a safe and supportive environment for these activities. Providing opportunities for sensory exploration can help high-functioning autistic toddlers learn and grow.

Calming Techniques

Children with autism frequently experience a constant state of "fight-or-flight," making it difficult for them to control their emotional and behavioral reactions. Teaching toddlers specific skills such as recognizing triggers and the early signs of sensory or emotional overload can help them develop effective self-regulation. A sensory overload in autistic toddlers may put them in a constant state of "fight-or-flight," but there are methods that can be used to help soothe an autistic child. Even highly functioning toddlers can "melt down" in situations that would be only marginally difficult for a typical child.

One effective calming technique for high-functioning autistic toddlers is the use of a weighted blanket or lap pad. These items provide deep pressure and a sense of security, which can help to calm an overstimulated child. Another technique is to provide a quiet and comfortable space for the child to retreat to when they are feeling overwhelmed. This can be a designated "calm down corner" with soft lighting and sensory toys, such as a soft blanket and a stuffed animal. It is also important to establish a routine and predictability in the child's environment to help reduce anxiety and provide a sense of control. Additionally, deep breathing exercises and mindfulness techniques can be taught and practiced to help the child regulate their emotions and manage stress.

Movement

Autistic toddlers have significant motor delays that worsen with age when compared to typically developing toddlers. The assessment of these toddlers' motor development is critical because motor delay in ASD toddlers is more pronounced in older toddlers. Enrolling your toddler in a sport or dance class, going on walks with them, or even playing energetic games with them can help them get the activity they require. Autistic toddlers may lag behind their peers in gross motor abilities by six months and in fine motor skills by a year. Early detection of motor delays may enable the administration of early intervention treatments. Exercise can aid in the reduction of anxiety, the improvement of focus, and the development of healthy coping mechanisms.

High-functioning autistic toddlers are able to attend mainstream schools and participate in typical activities. They may exhibit unique behaviors and challenges, such as difficulty with social interactions and sensory processing. Advocates are pushing for more specialized resources and support for these toddlers and their families. They also advocate for greater acceptance and understanding of autism in general. The movement for high-functioning autistic toddlers is gaining momentum as more parents and advocates are recognizing the unique needs and potential of these toddlers. These toddlers are on the autism spectrum but have relatively normal communication and cognitive abilities. With the right resources and support, these toddlers can go on to lead fulfilling and successful lives.

Sorting

You can help your toddler sort and organize their belongings by purchasing storage containers, labeling everything, and instructing them on how to store things in an organized manner. As a result, they will develop the habit of staying organized and maintaining a clean environment. Individuals with autism are significantly more likely to sort using a specific criterion than those without the disorder. Sorting is an excellent way for people on the autism spectrum to work on developing skills. Although people with autism may be more concerned with how things are classified, everything can be classified based on different characteristics. Many toddlers with HFA benefit from having a place for everything, which can help with anxiety and promote positive coping skills.

Sorting activities can be beneficial for high-functioning autistic toddlers as they can help improve their organization skills and attention to detail. These activities can also help with visual perception and discrimination, as well as enhancing their fine motor skills. Examples of sorting activities include sorting objects by size, shape, color, or texture. These activities can be done with everyday objects such as toys, blocks, or even food items. It is important to make the activity fun and engaging for the child, and to provide support and guidance as needed. By incorporating sorting activities into their routine, high-functioning autistic toddlers can improve their cognitive abilities and develop essential skills for daily life.

Creativity

Many who are diagnosed with autism struggle to put their experiences into context. When asked to list as many applications as they can for an everyday item, people with more autistic characteristics offer fewer ideas. Their proposals, however, are more atypical when compared to those of their neurotypical colleagues. Creativity and imagination may be particularly strong among autistic toddlers. Children can use tools to sketch, paint, or play an instrument to exercise their motor skills while creating art in both unstructured and structured ways. Resourcefulness is an important trait for self-sufficient people, and creativity can help foster it. The sense of accomplishment that comes from completing an artistic project is another benefit that can boost confidence and self-esteem.

One way to encourage creativity in high-functioning autistic toddlers is to provide them with a variety of materials to explore and manipulate. This could include art supplies such as crayons, markers, and paint, as well as tactile materials like playdough and sand. Providing clear instructions and demonstrations can also help them understand how to use the materials and create their own unique creations. Encouraging them to express themselves through art, music, or movement can also provide an outlet for their creativity. Creating a supportive and accepting environment where they feel safe to experiment and express themselves will foster their natural creative abilities.

Chapter 4: Promoting Language and Communication Skills

HFA toddlers can communicate in a variety of ways, just like anyone else. Some may use speech to communicate, while others may use alternative forms of communication such as sign language, gestures, or communication boards. Some high-functioning autistic kids may also use assistive technology such as speech-generating devices or apps to help them communicate.

Parents can help improve their child's communication skills by providing a supportive and communicative environment at home. This can include using clear and consistent language, providing opportunities for their child to practice communicating, and offering support and encouragement. It can also be helpful for parents to learn about their child's specific communication needs and preferences, and to work with therapists or other professionals to develop a communication plan that meets those needs. Additionally, using visual aids and other forms of support, such as social stories, can be helpful for some toddlers with autism.

Communication and Autism in Children

Communication skills are one of the most important components of social interaction and communication for neurotypical people; however, these skills may need to be learned for people with autism spectrum disorders. Children with autism may feel as if the odds are stacked against them when it comes to learning verbal and nonverbal communication skills.

Children with autism spectrum disorders (ASD) are frequently self-absorbed and segregated. They may struggle to learn a language and understand what others are saying to them. Many people have difficulty with word meaning and phrase flow. They may also be unable to understand facial expressions, distinct verbal tones, and body language.

These youngsters frequently struggle with communication because they may struggle to grasp and express their thoughts and emotions. Scripts and repetition are one way high-functioning autistic youngsters communicate. They may use certain language or behaviors to express their thoughts and feelings. A child, for example, may repeatedly say the words "I am happy" to indicate their satisfaction.

Nonverbal clues such as gestures, facial expressions, and body language are another way high-functioning autistic toddlers communicate. Even if they are unable to communicate themselves verbally, nonverbal cues can help them explain their emotions and thoughts. High-functioning autistic youngsters, on the other hand, may fail to grasp and interpret nonverbal cues from others. This can lead to misconceptions and disruptions in communication. A youngster, for example, may not comprehend why another person is sobbing and may be unsure how to respond or soothe them.

As a parent, you must understand the particular ways in which your high-functioning autistic kid communicates and provide support and direction to help them improve their communication skills. Providing a regulated and predictable setting is one strategy to improve your toddler's communication abilities. This can make your youngster more at ease and confident in expressing themselves. It can also assist them in comprehending and interpreting nonverbal messages from others.

When it comes to language skills, some toddlers with ASD are actually ahead of their neurotypical peers. These toddlers may possess a vocabulary beyond their years, or use language in a formal, almost businesslike manner. Often these toddlers are skilled at memorizing the rules of language; they may therefore be particularly good at spelling and learning new words. However, the application and everyday use of language for social interaction could be challenging for them.

How Autism Affects Toddlers' Communication Skills

Autism is a neurodevelopmental disorder that affects a person's ability to communicate and interact with others. Children with autism may have difficulty with verbal and nonverbal communication, such as making eye contact, using gestures, and understanding and using language to express their thoughts and ideas. They may also have difficulty with social interactions and may not understand social cues, such as tone of voice and body language. Additionally, they might struggle to comprehend and make use of verbal cues like gestures and spoken language. They might have a hard time looking you in the eye. They might favor using alternative communication techniques, like sign language or picture books.

Communication difficulties are common in high-functioning autistic toddlers. They might have a hard time reading nonverbal cues like facial expressions and body language. Children with HFA frequently have specialized interests in particular topics and can be extremely knowledgeable about those topics. Due to this, high-functioning autistic toddlers may come off as distant or uninterested in other people. But a lot of high-functioning autistic kids are actually very interested in interacting with other people, even though they might not know how to start or carry on a conversation.

It's interesting to note that typically developing toddlers begin to use more speech and speech-like sound combinations at around 15 months. Because these sounds and words are recognizable, it encourages parents to respond more frequently, which increases the chances for back-and-forth conversations. However, speech development is frequently delayed in toddlers on the autism spectrum. Their parents may have fewer opportunities to respond because they aren't receiving the same feedback from them, which could result in fewer conversations in general.

One of the most significant challenges for toddlers with autism is their difficulty with language and communication. Many toddlers with autism do not develop speech and language skills at the same rate as their peers, and may have delays in their ability to use and understand words. Some toddlers with autism may have a limited vocabulary and may have difficulty using language to express their thoughts and ideas. They may also have difficulty with the inflection and tone of their voice, which can make it difficult for others to understand what they are trying to say.

They may also have difficulty with imaginative play and may not understand the concept of taking turns or sharing. This can make it difficult for them to interact with their peers and may lead to social isolation. Overall, autism affects toddlers' communication skills in many ways. They may have difficulty with language and speech, and may have challenges with social interactions. However, with early intervention and support, toddlers with autism can learn to overcome these challenges and develop their communication skills.

Why Communication Skills Are Important for High-Functioning Autistic Toddlers

Children with autism must learn communication skills if they are to develop normally. Behavior, learning, and socialization are all aided by them. Children with autism need assistance in order to learn how to communicate. For people to express their needs, wants, feelings, and emotions, communication is crucial. It is crucial for social interaction and establishing bonds with others.

Many challenging behaviors are influenced by communication difficulties. Children may use less socially acceptable methods to satisfy needs if they don't know how to communicate them appropriately. Developing communication skills can aid in preventing and reducing problematic behaviors.

It's essential for relationships: High-functioning autistic toddlers often have difficulty communicating with others, which can make it difficult for them to form and maintain relationships. Without effective communication, it can be difficult to express needs and wants, understand others, and build rapport.

It's necessary for learning: In order to learn, high-functioning autistic toddlers need to be able to communicate effectively. Without being able to communicate, they may have difficulty understanding instructions, participating in class, and asking questions.

It's important for safety: Being able to communicate effectively can help high-functioning autistic toddlers stay safe in potentially dangerous situations: If they are unable to communicate their needs or understand the instructions of others, they may be at risk of injury or harm.

It's essential for managing emotions: Difficulty communicating can lead to frustration and emotional outbursts in high-functioning autistic toddlers. If they can't express how they are feeling or understand the emotions of others, they may become overwhelmed and act out in negative ways.

It's key for social interactions: Without effective communication skills, high-functioning autistic toddlers may have trouble making friends and participating in social activities. They may appear aloof or uninterested in others, which can make it difficult to connect with them on a social level.

It's necessary for success in life: Effective communication is essential for success in all areas of life, from school to work to personal relationships. High-functioning autistic toddlers who are unable to communicate effectively will likely struggle in many areas of their lives.

In order for your toddler to realize his or her potential, you, as a parent, want to give them every chance. Being able to communicate is a necessity in life, but it can be difficult for kids with autism spectrum disorders. You can get help from experts like speech-language pathologists and other educators to achieve the communication goals you've set for your toddler. Keep in mind that you are your toddler's most important and reliable adult during their formative years because you are the one who knows them best and cares about them the most.

How Children With Autism Communicate

Children with autism communicate in many different ways. Some toddlers with autism use words to communicate, while others may use gestures or body language. Some communicate using a combination of words and gestures. Some use assistive devices to help them communicate. Some communicate through their behavior. All toddlers with autism are unique and will communicate in their own way.

Repetitive or rigid language: Some toddlers with autism spectrum disorder say things that are meaningless or unrelated to the conversations they are having. Some autistic toddlers have high-pitched, sing-song voices or communicate robotically. Echolalia causes toddlers to repeat words they have heard. A child may, for example, count from one to five while engaging in a conversation unrelated to numbers. "Do you want something to eat?" the child may respond when asked if they want to eat. Other kids might start a conversation with cliché introductions like, "I am Mark."

Narrow interests and exceptional abilities: 10% of toddlers with ASD have "savant" talents, or very high aptitudes in particular fields like math, music, calendar computation, or memory. Some toddlers are capable of creating a thorough monologue about a topic that grabs their interest. Others may have exceptional mathematical and counting abilities or musical talent.

Uneven language development: Though not always at a typical level, many autistic toddlers do acquire some speech and language abilities. Before the age of five, some people may be able to read words, but they might not understand what they have read. As a result, it's sometimes believed that these kids have hearing issues. Many kids can recall details they've recently heard or seen with ease.

Poor nonverbal conversation skills: Children with autism frequently lack the ability to elucidate their speech with gestures. Many ASD toddlers find it difficult to express themselves when they lack meaningful gestures or other nonverbal skills to support their oral language abilities. They might express their annoyance through inappropriate behaviors or loud outbursts.

Tips for Communicating With Your Autistic Toddler

Another way to improve your toddler's communication skills is to model appropriate communication and social skills. This can include using clear and concise language, maintaining eye contact, and using gestures and facial expressions to convey emotions. By modeling these skills, your toddler can learn to use them in their own communication.

It is also important to provide your toddler with opportunities to practice their communication skills. This can include role-playing different social situations, such as making introductions or asking for help. It can also include providing your toddler with social stories, which are written or visual explanations of social rules and expectations.

Additionally, seeking support from a speech therapist or other professionals can be beneficial in improving your toddler's communication skills. These professionals can provide personalized strategies and techniques to help your toddler improve their communication abilities.

These are general tips you can use when focusing on building communication skills with your toddler:

Use short, simple sentences: When you are speaking to your HFA toddler, use short, simple sentences. Long and drawn out conversations can be distracting and cause potential for a loss of focus. Short and simple sentences will help them understand what you are saying and make it easier for them to respond. You allow them to process information better and hold the communication necessary to have a conversation.

Make eye contact: Make sure to make eye contact with your toddler when you are speaking to them. This will help them feel more engaged in the conversation. It pulls their focus in and provides them with the opportunity to pay attention to what is being said.

Repeat back what they say: When your toddler speaks, repeat back what they say. This will help them to know that you are listening and that you understand them. By allowing your toddler to lead the activity, they will be more motivated to stay in the interaction and potentially send you a message about what they're interested in.

Prompt them to respond: If your toddler is having trouble responding, prompt them by asking questions or giving choices. For example, you could ask, "Do you want to wear the blue skirt or the green skirt?" Your response should follow whatever message your toddler sent. Putting your toddler's message into words with these types of short comments gives them the language that describes their interests, and it also lets them know you understand their message and want to keep the conversation going. After you respond, look at them again and wait again to see if they send another message.

Use facial expressions and gestures: In addition to speaking, use facial expressions and gestures to communicate with your toddler. It will help them understand what you are saying and make it more fun for them!

Be patient: It often takes a child with ASD longer to process information. You may need to slow down your conversation to their speed. Long pauses can be helpful. Communicating with a high-functioning autistic toddler can be challenging, so be patient! If they don't understand something, try again in a different way. With time and practice, they will develop the communication skills they need.

Oftentimes, toddlers with ASD need extra time to take in what you are saying or to think about what they want to say in return. Slow down the pace of your conversation and say less. Use keywords or repeat important information. Pause more often between words and sentences, and try not to use too many questions.

Activities to Help Your Autistic Child Develop Communication Skills

Interaction occurs whenever you and your toddler do things together and respond to one another. Every time you and your toddler interact, you make a connection that gets communication started. In order to have successful interactions, your toddler needs to respond to others and initiate interactions on his/her own.

Communication is not always verbal in nature. Look at how your toddler communicates. Do they cry or scream? Do they move their body when they are next to people or things? Point at things? Make sounds? Look at things they want? Use words or sentences? Use echolalia or repeat what you say? Just as his or her form of communication may be different at various times, he or she will communicate for different reasons. He or she may be protesting or refusing, requesting, responding, trying to get your attention, greet or say good-bye, ask questions, express feelings, etc.

Your child's communication will depend on his/her ability to interact with you. Additionally, their communication will depend on how he or she communicates, and why he or she is communicating. It will also depend on your toddler's level of understanding. It is important to know what your toddler can and cannot do.

Use picture books: One way to help your toddler develop communication skills is to use picture books. Picture books can help to teach your toddler new words and concepts. You can also use picture books to model appropriate social behaviors, such as turn-taking and sharing.

Play games: Playing games is another great way to help your toddler develop communication skills. Games such as *Simon Says* and *I Spy* can help improve your toddler's listening skills. Games that involve taking turns, such as *Candyland* or *Chutes and Ladders*, can also help your toddler practice communicating with others.

Use puppets: Puppets are a great tool for helping toddlers with autism develop communication skills: Puppets can be used to model appropriate social behaviors, such as turn-taking and sharing; puppets can also be used to teach new words and concepts.

Engage in pretend play: Pretend play is another activity that can help your toddler develop communication skills. Pretend play helps toddlers practice using language in a meaningful way. It also helps toddlers understand others' perspectives and learn about emotions.

Use sign language: Using sign language is a great way to help your toddler communicate before they are able to use spoken language. Sign language can also be used alongside spoken language to help your toddler communicate more effectively. When words don't come easily, gestures can help. ASD kids might develop their own series of gestures to communicate. If this is the case, it's best to learn their language and follow their lead. Chances are, gestures come naturally to the child.

Use visual aids: Consider assistive devices and visual supports. Assistive technologies and visual supports can do more than take the place of speech. They can foster its development. Visual supports, such as pictures or symbols or even their favorite objects, can be very helpful for toddlers with autism who are trying to communicate. Visual supports can help your toddler understand what you are saying and can also provide a way for them to communicate their own needs and wants.

Encourage vocalizations: Encouraging your toddler to make sounds, even if they are not yet using words, is important for helping them develop communication skills. Vocalizations can help your toddler learn about the sounds of language and how they are used to form words. Additionally, vocalizations can be a first step toward using spoken language.

Read aloud together: Reading aloud together is a great way for you and your toddler to bond while also helping them develop communication skills. Reading aloud helps toddlers learn about the structure of language and how words are used to form sentences. Additionally, listening to you read aloud can help your toddler develop their own reading skills.

In conclusion, HFA toddlers may have difficulty with communication, but with support and guidance from parents, they can improve their communication skills. By providing a structured and predictable environment, modeling appropriate communication and social skills, providing opportunities for practice, and seeking support from professionals, parents can help their HFA toddler become more confident and effective communicators.

Chapter 5: Practicing Play

Your HFA toddler needs play in order to develop, so if you don't include it in their daily activities, you're missing out on a critical stage. Play is fundamentally about interacting. That meeting must first be designed to facilitate dialogue and education. Toys serve as backdrops for play-based interactions. Toys don't have to be elaborate; they can simply be a box, blanket, feather, pillow, etc.

Why do autistic toddlers have more difficulty playing pretend than typically developing toddlers? A number of hypotheses have been proposed in response to the delays or differences that toddlers with autism exhibit in pretend play. Researchers have also looked into a variety of abilities to see if they contribute to the development of pretend play.

How Children With Autism Tend to Play

Children with autism play differently than other toddlers due to differences in brain development that prevent them from functioning normally. Instead of pretending to be someone else, they frequently choose to perform actions and arrange items repeatedly. Children with autism may also ignore or act as if they are unaware that other toddlers are nearby or in the same space as them. Autistic toddlers may not be interested in games that require "make believe" or pretending to be someone, something, or somewhere else. They prefer to play alone in general. There are numerous therapies available to assist autistic toddlers and their families in playing and developing relationships.

These are some of the behaviors they may exhibit and how they may manifest in play:

Repetitive behaviors: Engaging in activities that seem purposeless and repetitive. Examples include opening and closing doors, lining up objects, and flushing the toilet. Autistic toddlers may repetitively play with the same toys or engage in the same activities. Autistic toddlers also often engage in repetitive behaviors during play, such as spinning, rocking, or hand-flapping. This is because they find comfort in the predictability and routine of these activities.

Sensory issues: Autistic toddlers may also have Sensory Processing Disorder, which means that they are either hypersensitive or hyposensitive to certain stimuli. For example, they may be bothered by loud noises or bright lights, or they may seek out sensory input by constantly touching objects or spinning in circles.

Difficulty with social interactions: A preference for playing alone almost all the time. This can happen even when encouraged to participate in typical forms of play. Autistic toddlers often prefer to play alone rather than with other toddlers. or have difficulty interacting with other toddlers. They may not make eye contact or engage in reciprocal conversations. Instead, they may prefer to play alone or engage in parallel play, where they play side-by-side but not with each other. Autistic toddlers may not engage in imaginative play, such as pretend games.

Unusual interests: Autistic toddlers may be more interested in objects than people. Autistic toddlers may also exhibit unusual interests, such as a fascination with a particular subject or object. They may spend hours playing with the same toy or watching the same movie over and over again.

Delayed speech and language development: Autistic toddlers may have difficulty understanding social cues and body language. They may have differences in motor skills. Autistic toddlers often have difficulty with change and transitions. They may become upset if their routine is disrupted or if they are introduced to new people or places. This is because they like predictability and feel safest when things stay the same. Autistic toddlers may also have special talents or abilities, such as an extraordinary memory or an aptitude for music or math, though not always.

Why Do Autistic Children Play Differently?

Autism presents itself in different ways and each child has capabilities unique to them. However, research regarding play and autism has narrowed it down to a few possibilities which could be the cause. By working on these skills together with your HFA child, you provide them the opportunity to achieve milestones for progressive development in the future.

Lack of Joint Attention Skills

It is likely that joint attention and pretend play will interact. Joint attention behaviors include pointing to emphasize, share, or demonstrate interest in an object, as well as using alternate eye contact to see if others are paying attention to the same thing or event as them. It's possible that autistic toddlers' lack of joint attention abilities hamper the development of pretend play. Joint attention skills are required for effective play, and pretend play helps toddlers develop these skills. According to a longitudinal study, joint attention abilities are critical for the development of pretend play in both typically developing and developmentally delayed toddlers.

Joint attention requires two components:

- Two people need to share an interest in an object (a toy) or an event (watching a soccer game).

- The same two people must understand that they are both interested in the same object or event.

The majority of average toddlers have innately learned the fundamentals of joint attention by the age of 18 months. Most autistic toddlers lack the motivation to learn this skill because they are not "wired" to interact with others in this manner. Furthermore, toddlers with ASDs lack the typical social referencing abilities. The ability to interpret a person's facial expressions is referred to as social referencing. It can be difficult for autistic toddlers to play with other toddlers because they cannot tell how someone is feeling based on their facial expression.

Having trouble using pragmatic language and other related social skills

The social use of language, including nonverbal cues like body language, is known as social pragmatics. It encompasses both what we say and how we say it (tone of voice). Knowing social pragmatics also aids in understanding conversational turn--taking, or when to speak and when to let others speak. Additional features of social pragmatics include

- deciphering figurative language

- emotional expression and interpretation

- being receptive to the opinions and suggestions of others

- resolving issues

It is challenging for autistic toddlers to comprehend others' intentions and respond appropriately because they struggle with most, if not all, of the four major play skills listed earlier. It can also be challenging for them to make friends, leading to social exclusion, isolation, and even bullying, since they don't have the same desire to interact with or communicate with potential playmates as typically developing kids do.

Lack of Generativity

Children with autism may experience difficulties producing pretend play due to generativity problems, such as difficulties in generating new ideas and actions that are needed during pretend play. During free play periods, they are less likely than typically developing toddlers to engage in acts of pretend play spontaneously. However, this does not mean that they do not have the ability to engage in pretend play. Studies that provide instructions for toddlers to pretend find that toddlers with autism do have the ability to engage in pretend play. Thus, the reduction in the production of pretense during play lies in the difficulty with generating ideas or self-initiated actions for toddlers with autism.

Additionally, some researchers have hypothesized that the difficulties or delays that toddlers with autism face with pretend play may be due to a lack of imitation skills. However, studies have found that imitation skills are unrelated to the development of pretend play. Other researchers have hypothesized that the deficits in meta-representational skills may interfere with the pretend play development of toddlers with autism.

A lack of meta-representational skills means that toddlers with autism may have difficulties "representing how another represents the world," which also indicates a global inability to engage in pretend play. Contrary to the meta-representational deficit explanation, toddlers are able to produce pretend play under certain circumstances, such as when there are prompts for them to engage in pretend play. Hence, research evidence shows that the lack of meta-representational skills does not explain the deficits in pretend play for toddlers with autism.

Why Play Is Particularly Important for Autistic Children

Because play is such an important part of raising toddlers, we frequently overlook its importance in so many aspects of a child's development. Play teaches toddlers a variety of important skills for future development. Many toddlers with autism spectrum disorders have skill deficiencies and disruptive behavioral behaviors that prevent them from engaging in developmentally appropriate play.

Many autistic toddlers' games may be different and more difficult. You are eager to engage in play and conversation with your toddlers. Your efforts to participate as a parent may occasionally fall short.

However, with patience and encouragement, they should be able to advance in their game. To accomplish this, you must encourage their "social play," which will also promote other aspects of their development.

Play generally falls into one of six categories and progresses in these ways:

- exploratory play

- cause-and-effect play

- toy play

- constructive play

- physical play

- pretend play

You can aid in your toddler's learning and practice of new skills and abilities while also assisting in the development of their play. The overall development of your toddler depends on these abilities. They include the capacity to observe the environment, imitate others, share items, take turns, speculate about the thoughts and feelings of others, communicate, and more.

The following crucial play skills may suffer as a result of these challenges:

- copying simple actions

- exploring the environment

- sharing objects and attention with others

- responding to others

- taking turns

Benefits of Play for Autistic Toddlers

Social Interaction

Promoting social skills naturally is crucial when parenting toddlers with autism. Play is a fantastic way to practice skills like attention, sharing, and communication. Playing one-on-one with your toddler or encouraging interaction between your toddler and other friends or siblings are both effective ways to help them develop these skills. As your toddler plays, remind them to share the toys with others, wait to take toys from others, etc.

Play can aid in the development of social skills in autistic toddlers, which is one of its advantages. Children can practice social skills such as sharing, taking turns, and resolving conflicts through play. Furthermore, as they practice communicating their needs and wants to others, toddlers can improve their communication skills through play.

Physical Activity

Toddlers with ASD also benefit from play in getting the necessary exercise. Many autistic kids struggle to tolerate particular kinds of physical activity due to sensory issues. They can, however, partake in physical activity in a way that is entertaining and stimulating to them through play. Exercise also helps the cardiovascular system, builds bones and muscles, and lowers stress levels, to name just a few of its many health advantages.

Cognitive Development

Executive abilities such as self-control and mental flexibility, as well as cognitive and linguistic ability, all influence how play develops and is used in clinical settings. Autism affects all of these areas. In toddlers without autism, the ability to pretend play is more closely related to self-control measures than cognitive ability (learning and memory).

Play is also important for the cognitive development of autistic toddlers. Children have the opportunity to explore, experiment, and discover new things about their surroundings through play. This stimulates their minds and can help them improve their problem-solving and critical thinking abilities. As they learn how to come up with new ideas and solutions, toddlers can develop creative thinking skills.

Even in toddlers who are barely speaking, play appears to correlate with language skills and IQ in autistic toddlers. Preschool play abilities can predict these toddlers' later linguistic development. Differences in normal preschoolers' ability to act out scenarios and suspend disbelief are related to how well they perform on tasks requiring patience or the selection of an illogical solution.

Emotional Development

Children develop self-regulation skills, particularly in social and supervised play, by adhering to rules and paying attention despite emotions such as anticipation or irritation. Through play, toddlers learn how to make and adjust rules, as well as when to take the lead and when to follow.

Using this technique, toddlers can express their feelings through pretend play without having to claim them as their own. Create one-of-a-kind play environments and scenarios with your parents and siblings. Pretend play can also help toddlers deal with their strong emotions as a result of their upsetting circumstances.

Play can also assist autistic toddlers in their emotional development. Toddlers can express themselves through play in a safe and controlled environment. This can assist them in understanding and coping with their emotions in a healthy manner. Play can also provide a sense of joy and happiness, which can help with emotional development.

Reducing Stress Levels

Another advantage of play for autistic toddlers is that it might aid in stress reduction. Because of the difficulties they face in their daily lives, many autistic toddlers feel significant levels of stress. They can, however, take a break from these trials and relax both physically and psychologically by playing. Furthermore, play can aid in the release of endorphins, which are chemicals that have mood-boosting properties.

This is due to the fact that they have distinct beginning and ending points and provide toddlers with specific instructions on what to do when. They might gain a better understanding of the techniques, abilities, tasks, or concepts necessary to achieve the desired result. It makes games and play activities more predictable and controllable for toddlers with autism. All of this contributes to a less stressful environment in which your toddler can practice the skills needed to play and interact with other toddlers.

Tips for Helping Your Autistic Toddler Develop Play Skills

1) **Encourage Imagination:** Imagination is one of the finest methods to help your child develop play skills. You may accomplish this by giving kids open-ended toys that can be utilized in a variety of ways, such as blocks, dolls, and puzzles. You can also foster their imagination by telling them stories and allowing them to make up their own.

2) **Encourage Pretend Play:** Pretend play is a vital element of toddler development since it helps them grasp their surroundings. To encourage pretend play, provide your child with props such as toy phones, kitchen sets,

and dress-up clothes. Create pretend play scenarios for your toddler to act out, such as going to the grocery store or going to the doctor.

3) **Encourage Physical Activity:** Physical play is rough-and-tumble play, running around and so on. This type of play gives your toddler whole-body exercise and helps them develop gross motor skills. Physical activity is important for toddlers of all ages, and it can also help to develop play skills. You can encourage physical activity by providing your toddler with toys that encourage movement, such as balls, jump ropes, and tricycles. You can also take your toddler outside to play games or go for walks.

4) **Encourage Social Interaction:** Social interaction is another important part of play and child development. You can encourage social interaction by providing your toddler with toys that require two or more people to play, such as board games, card games, and puzzles. You can also take your toddler to playgrounds or other places where they can interact with other toddlers.

5) **Be a Good Role Model:** It's important to be a good role model for your toddler when it comes to play. This means playing with your toddler yourself and showing them how much fun it can be. It also means being patient and

not getting frustrated if they don't understand a game or if they lose interest quickly.

6) **Teach Turn-Taking:** If you want to help your toddler develop play skills, it is important to teach them how to take turns. This skill is important not only in games and other activities but also in everyday life. You can teach your toddler how to take turns by modeling the behavior yourself and providing opportunities for practice.

7) **Encourage Communication:** Encouraging communication is another great way to help your toddler develop play skills. You can do this by modeling communication yourself and encouraging your toddler to express themselves through words, sounds, and gestures. Additionally, you can provide opportunities for your toddler to practice communicating by playing games that require communication, such as charades or Simon Says.

8) **Have Fun:** Above all else, remember to have fun! Playing with your toddler should be enjoyable for both of you. If you're feeling stressed or overwhelmed, take a break and come back when you're both feeling refreshed.

Chapter 6: Bonding With Your Child

When discussing your parental response to your special-needs child, bonding is critical. You must comprehend the importance of bonding and how it may affect your kids' emotional health.

Bonding is the process of establishing a strong emotional bond between a parent and a toddler. It entails the formation of a deep emotional relationship between the two, as well as the transmission of familial ties that enable comprehension and nonverbal communication. Bonding is characterized by a parent's everlasting affection for their child and is an important stage in assisting the toddler in developing a healthy sense of their own value and self-worth. Bonding also contributes to a child's sense of security, as evidenced by the mutual concern and love that both parents and toddlers have for one another.

Bonding also serves as a technique for integrating a toddler into the parent's extended family, providing them with a sense of family attachment as well as a larger web of love and care. Bonding is a crucial part of parenting and is necessary for a toddler's healthy development and well-being. It enables the formation of an emotional tie between a parent and child, which is a vital basis for the development of strong and healthy relationships.

Autism spectrum disorder (ASD) toddlers frequently struggle with relationships and communication. Families with ASD toddlers face numerous challenges. A strong emphasis on consistency and communication may bring the entire family closer together. Difficulties can range from failing to recognize social advances to serious communication skills deficiencies, which can lead to social anxiety. Parents of autistic toddlers may find it difficult to form close relationships with them. It is critical to maintain close ties and open conversations throughout an autistic toddler's development.

How Autism Affects Bonding

Autistic toddlers often have difficulty bonding with others, which can make it difficult for them to form close relationships. This can be due to a number of factors, including trouble understanding and responding to social cues. HFA toddlers may prefer to be alone or engage in repetitive behaviors rather than interact with others. Some toddlers with ASD may be hypersensitive to touch, sound, or other stimuli, which can make it difficult for them to tolerate being close to others. They may have difficulty understanding the emotions of others, which can make it difficult to bond with them.

Social interaction development is severely and widely

impaired in toddlers with autism spectrum disorder. This may have an impact on both parenting and the attachment bond with their parents. In research conducted by Rutgers et al. (2007), parents of neurotypical toddlers reported higher levels of authoritative parenting than parents of ASD toddlers and parents of neurodivergent toddlers.

The inability to bond with others can have a significant impact on development. Without strong bonds, toddlers may have difficulty developing a sense of self-worth and may struggle to form healthy relationships later in life. Additionally, a lack of bonding can lead to social isolation and anxiety.

The Benefits of Bonding for High-Functioning Autistic Toddlers

It Helps Them Connect With Others: When you take the time to cuddle, play, and talk with your toddler, you are helping them develop the social skills that they need to interact with other people. Plus, bonding with your toddler will help them feel more comfortable in social situations and will make it easier for them to make friends.

It Reduces Anxiety and Stress: Many autistic toddlers experience high levels of anxiety, which can be exacerbated by social situations. Bonding with your toddler will help them feel more secure and will allow them to better cope with stressful situations.

It Increases Their Self-Esteem: When you show your toddler affection and attention, you are helping them feel good about themselves. Additionally, as your toddler grows and develops, they will be able to look back on the time spent bonding with you and feel proud of their accomplishments.

It Teaches Them Important Life Skills: Bonding with your HFA toddler is also important because it can help them learn important life skills. For example, through playtime and conversation, your toddler will learn how to communicate effectively with others. Additionally, they will learn how to express their emotions in a healthy way and how to resolve conflict in a constructive manner.

It Strengthens the Parent–Child Relationship: Finally, bonding with your HFA toddler is important because it strengthens the parent-child relationship. When you take the time to connect with your toddler on a deeper level, you are creating a foundation of trust and respect that will last a lifetime. Additionally, bonding with your toddler will make it easier for you to understand their needs and how best to support them.

How HFA Toddlers Like to Bond

HFA toddlers like to bond through shared interests. They often have a keen interest in a particular subject, and they may want to share this with you. They may also like to bond through physical activities such as swimming or running. They may be very good at art or music, and they may want to share their talents with you. They may also like to bond by discussing their interests with you. They may also enjoy spending time with you doing everyday activities such as shopping or going for a walk.

Some parents struggle to comprehend how they can bond with their autistic child. The range is broad, with some toddlers nonverbal and others high-functioning. You'll still love your toddler as much as you did before the diagnosis, but you'll need to know the answers to some basic questions.

Don't Make Assumptions: To understand what an autistic child is feeling and thinking, pay close attention to their body language and facial expressions. Children with autism frequently have a straight face and flat tones, deviating from accepted standards of emotional expression. You won't have to put in much effort to figure out whether your toddler is happy, sad, or about to have a meltdown.

Initiate Play: If your toddler has difficulty expressing their desire to play, you must make an effort to assist them. Use signs and other items to help guide them to some playtime with you. Signs and other items can be used to direct them toward some play. Use a visual chart that shows the time of day to see what's coming up. Using visual charts that combine words and images, your toddler can understand the purpose of each block of time.

Use the Right Words: Although it will take time, you can begin teaching your toddler sarcasm right away. Make a note of any words or phrases that you use to avoid confusing toddlers. Autistic toddlers frequently express themselves in extremely literal ways. When attempting to establish a close relationship with your toddler, use clear and concise language. If you tell them to "get a move on," which is code for "hurry up," they might start moving weirdly or even dance. This means that you should avoid using sarcasm and other expressions that you are used to using.

Find Their Interests: You should pay attention to what your toddler is interested in. Some unfamiliar shows, toys, and other pastimes may pique your toddler's interest to the point of obsession. The time has come for you to learn about your toddler's interests. If your toddler enjoys watching anime or playing specific video games, you might want to consider learning these activities alongside them. You can use this in a variety of ways to improve your relationship with your toddler.

It all comes down to learning how to strengthen your bond with your toddler by paying attention to their cues, interests, and responses. Once you understand what motivates your toddler, you'll be able to come up with creative ways to spend quality time with them without conflict.

Tips for Bonding With Your Toddler

There are no hard-and-fast rules on how to communicate with an HFA toddler, but many families have had success with the following tips.

Get on Their Level: This means getting down on the floor and playing with them at their level. Try to engage them in activities that they enjoy, such as building blocks or playing with cars. This will help them feel comfortable, which will make it easier for you to connect with them.

Make Eye Contact: This can be difficult, as many autistic toddlers do not like to make eye contact. However, it is important to try to do this as much as possible, as it will help them feel more connected to you. One way to make eye contact is to sit in front of them and let them see your face while you talk to them.

Use Simple Language: This means using short sentences and avoiding jargon or technical terms. You should also try to use words that they are familiar with and can understand. This will help them feel more comfortable and will make it easier for them to follow what you are saying.

Be Patient and Present: This means not getting frustrated if they do not respond the way you want them to or if they seem uninterested in what you are doing. It is important to remember that they are still learning how to interact with the world and that it takes time for them to adjust. Don't let your feelings get hurt if the child does not respond to you as you'd like. They can be blunt in their responses. Don't take this personally. Appreciate the time you're able to spend with your toddler in the moment.

Reward Good Behavior: A toddler with ASD may act badly at times to get you to focus on them. Ignoring this behavior is often the best way to prevent it. Also talk about and reward the child's good behavior often. One way to encourage good behavior in your HFA toddler is to reward them when they do something that you want them to do. This could be something as simple as giving them a sticker or playing their favorite song when they make eye contact or say a word correctly. This will help them understand that they are doing something that you approve of and will encourage them to continue doing it.

Stay Positive: Try not to get discouraged if they seem to be making progress slowly. HFA toddlers respond best to positive reinforcement. Be sure to talk about or reward good behavior often. Be generous with compliments for good behavior. Keep in mind that every child is different and that each one learns at their own pace. As long as you are patient and remain positive, they will eventually make progress.

Seek Professional Help: If you find that you are struggling to bond with your toddler, it may be helpful to seek professional help from a therapist or counselor who specializes in ASD. Don't be ashamed or worried that you cannot do something, you are not a failure. This just means you know when you need help. They will be able to give you specific tips and advice on how to best connect with your toddler.

Remember to Take Care of Yourself: Your ability to care for your toddler is dependent on how well you care for yourself. Give yourself a break from time to time and allow yourself the same patience you have with your little one. Join parent support groups. Or ask understanding family and friends to care for your toddler so you can recharge. School psychologists and counselors can also provide resources to help you.

Maintaining positive interaction with your HFA toddler can be challenging. However, it is one of the most important things you can do to assist your child in learning. According to research, early, frequent, and loving involvement by family members is one of the most effective ways to help toddlers with ASD.

Chapter 7: Encouraging Social Interaction

Our social skills govern our interactions with other people and with the outside world. In general, social skills are "learned" in the same way that linguistic skills are. People with autism may have a more difficult time learning and developing these skills, forcing them to make assumptions about how the social "map" should look.

Practicing social skills can increase participation in society and promote positive outcomes such as happiness and friendship. Many autistic toddlers and adults need help learning how to behave in different social situations. We gathered social skills advice from professionals, educators, and families, as well as practical tools to help improve opportunities for community participation.

Social skills development for people with autism involves

- focus on timing and attention

- learning behaviors that predict important social outcomes like friendship and happiness

- direct or explicit instruction and "teachable moments" with practice in realistic settings

- a way to build up cognitive and language skills

- support for enhancing communication and sensory integration

Autism and Socializing

According to the National Association of School Nurses (NASN, 2015), a child's development is dependent on their ability to feel comfortable in a variety of social situations. With strong social skills, your toddler can learn from others, make friends, and develop interests and hobbies. Furthermore, these skills can help strengthen family ties and give your toddler a sense of belonging.

Having social skills is one of the most important aspects of human life. Autism is characterized by difficulties with social interaction and repetitive behavior. As a result, toddlers with autism have a difficult time learning social skills. A lack of social skills may have an impact on a person's future life. If autistic toddlers are to participate in society, they must receive social skills interventions (Badiah, 2018).

Socializing improves the following skills in autistic toddlers:

- play skills—for example, taking turns in games or sharing toys

- conversation skills—for example, choosing what to talk about or what body language to use

- emotional skills—for example, managing emotions and understanding how others feel

- problem-solving skills—for example, dealing with conflict or making decisions in social situations

Many have difficulty understanding social cues. This can make it hard for them to know how to act in certain situations. Autistic toddlers may also have trouble reading other people's emotions. This can make it difficult for them to understand how someone is feeling and what they might be thinking.

Some often have difficulty understanding social cues and may not pick up on the nonverbal cues that people use to communicate, such as body language and facial expressions. This can make it hard for them to express themselves and understand what others are saying. They may also have trouble making eye contact, engaging in back-and-forth conversation, and taking turns in conversation.

Many prefer to be alone or engage in solitary activities. This can make it hard for them to interact with others and build relationships. Some may also exhibit repetitive or unusual behaviors, such as flapping their hands or rocking back and forth. This can make it difficult for them to interact with others, as they may be seen as strange or odd.

Many autistic toddlers have difficulty understanding or using gestures, which can again make it difficult for them to interact with others. This can be a particular problem in social situations where gestures are often used to communicate information such as turn-taking or agreement/disagreement.

How Autistic Toddlers Socialize

It's a common misconception that toddlers with autism do not make friends because they are antisocial. This is not the case. Children with autism want to make friends and talk to others, but they don't always know how to do it properly. They often struggle with being able to maintain eye contact and understand social interaction.

When someone says a child lacks social skills, it means he or she does not display expected behavior around other toddlers, making it harder to make friends. For instance, an autistic child might take another child's toy without asking for permission. This is viewed as negative behavior by most people, but a child with autism might not understand.

One-on-One Interactions: Autistic toddlers often prefer one-on-one interactions to group situations. This is because they can find large groups of people overwhelming and may have difficulty understanding all of the different social cues that are taking place. One-on-one interactions allow toddlers to take their time and process information at their own pace.

Small Groups: While autistic toddlers may prefer one-on-one interactions, they can also be successful in small group settings. This is because small groups provide a more manageable environment for them to navigate. Additionally, being in a small group allows toddlers to build relationships with a few other individuals, which can be beneficial for their social development.

Structured Activities: Autistic toddlers often thrive when they are involved in structured activities. This is because they like predictability and routine. Structured activities give toddlers a chance to practice their social skills in a safe and controlled setting.

Unstructured Playtime: While structured activities are important, autistic toddlers also need time to play without rules or expectations. This type of play allows them to explore their interests and use their imagination. It is also a great way for them to practice social skills such as turn-taking and sharing.

Technology: Many autistic toddlers enjoy using technology to socialize. This is because it can provide them with a way to connect with others who share their interests. Additionally, technology can be used to help facilitate communication for toddlers who have difficulty speaking or understanding spoken language.

Social skills are essential for a child to develop self-confidence, make friends, and get along with those around them. According to Barloso (2019), toddlers with ASD can build good relationships and gain life skills when they work on their social interactions. Autistic children need the same social skills as their neurotypical peers to succeed. They must learn responsibility, discipline, and the importance of arriving on time.

On a social level, a child with autism should learn to

- talk to others

- play with others (sharing, taking turns, pretend play)

- solve problems

- manage emotions

Once these basic skills are identified, it's easier to come up with a plan to improve a child's social skills.

Tips for Practicing Social Skills With Your Toddler

Regardless of where your child is on the autism spectrum, behavioral modification and social interaction should be heavily integrated into the child's life as early as possible. Social skills should be integrated into any and all behavioral plans. This is a dynamic and developmental process that must be maintained throughout your toddler's life. You must also take into account the child's physical, cognitive, emotional, and social development.

As a child grows through childhood and into adolescence, social demands and issues change dramatically, as does the individual's social interaction. In accordance with this, social intervention should also change. To address these issues, play dates, after-school activities with other toddlers, and social skills groups are highly recommended. The younger your child is when the social issue is addressed, the more proactive you should be in addressing the social issue. This, in turn, will have a positive impact on the child's life. These skills will also carry over into adolescence and adulthood.

No matter what modality or approach is used to treat ASD, a strong and dynamic social component should and must be integrated and implemented into the plan. This is critical for the individual to reach their full potential, form appropriate, nurturing, and positive relationships, and eventually lead an independent, productive, and happy life.

The following are a few ways in which you can help develop your toddler's social skills:

1) **Create a game out of it:** Games are an excellent tool for teaching social skills. Play out situations with your toddler. A toddler can learn anticipated and unexpected behavior in a particular setting via role-playing. While you act as the customer, your toddler can work the register. Allow your child to practice taking orders, managing cash, and dispensing change.

2) **Practice games:** It's a good idea to "practice" playing with a parent or sibling before sending a toddler out to play with others. You could explain how the game works and monitor your toddler's actions while playing.

3) **Utilize puppets:** Using puppets is a fantastic way to help your toddler develop social skills. Puppets can be used for role-playing, conversation, and scenario acting.

4) **Invest in a pet:** Research indicates that kids with autism who have pets are better able to develop their social skills. It's possible that interacting with animals improves people's social skills and capacity for friendship.

5) **Utilize technology:** Give your toddler access to tablet or smartphone apps to help them improve their communication skills, such as PECS. This will improve their social skills in turn.

6) **Practice in real-world settings:** It's crucial to practice social skills in both authentic and fictitious settings. Take your kid to a restaurant so they can practice placing an order and using the words please and thank you. If a child is anxious about a social activity, such as going to the dentist, you can watch videos of people or kids during a dental visit. It can also help the child recognize basic courtesy skills like greeting the doctor and following instructions.

7) **Give compliments:** A great way to promote positive social behavior is to give compliments. Make sure to compliment your toddler when they behave nicely or engage with others.

8) **Set an example of appropriate conduct for kids to follow:** Kids pick up on things from the people around them. Make sure to set a positive social example for your kids. This includes doing things like listening when others are speaking, using the words "please" and "thank you," and maintaining eye contact.

Chapter 8: Making Sense of Things

A person with autism may experience difficulties interpreting and organizing input from what they see, taste, touch, hear, and smell. Sensory perceptions can become frightening or even painful and can lead to high anxiety and meltdowns.

Due to sensory sensitivities, someone with autism might

- exhibit extraordinary sensory seeking behavior, such as smelling items or looking intensely at moving objects

- exhibit odd sensory avoidance behaviors, such as avoiding ordinary noises and textures such as hair dryers, clothing tags, vacuum cleaners, and sand

- demonstrate self-stimulatory actions, e.g., tapping their temples, fluttering their hands, hopping on their toes

- be so preoccupied with a favorite sensation or activity that they fail to perceive danger

Many people with autism show certain behaviors when they are experiencing a sensory issue:

- increased movement, such as jumping, whirling, or colliding with objects

- difficulty identifying internal feelings such as hunger, discomfort, or the urge to use the restroom

- refusing to eat or wear particular foods or garments

- chewing on non-food objects on a regular basis

- frequent touching of others or rough play

- covering one's ears or eyes

- difficulties talking or reacting when the brain reallocates resources to deal with sensory input (shutdown)

- stimming has increased, as seen by hand-flapping, repeated sounds, or rocking back and forth

- speaking more quickly and loudly, or not speaking at all

- escalating, overwhelming feelings, or the desire to flee a situation (meltdown)

How Autism Affects the Senses

Toddlers who have fully developed all seven senses are constantly exploring and learning about their surroundings through their senses. The development and education of a child are dependent on their ability to use their senses of sight, hearing, taste, smell, touch, balance, and bodily awareness. Caregivers must provide a variety of experiences and opportunities for toddlers to use and develop their senses in a safe and encouraging environment.

Toddlers with autism often experience difficulties with their seven senses, which include sight, hearing, taste, smell, touch, balance, and body awareness. These difficulties can manifest in various ways, such as an oversensitivity to certain stimuli or an undersensitivity to others. For example, a toddler with autism may have heightened sensitivity to loud noises, bright lights, or certain textures, leading to avoidance or distress when exposed to these stimuli.

On the other hand, they may have an underdeveloped sensitivity to pain or temperature, leading to self-injury or a lack of awareness of danger. Additionally, toddlers with autism may struggle with spatial awareness and body coordination, leading to difficulties with balance and gross motor skills. Overall, the seven senses can be significantly impacted in toddlers with autism, leading to challenges in daily life and the need for sensory integration therapy to help them better manage and regulate their sensory experiences.

This is known as hypersensitivity (over-responsiveness) and hyposensitivity (under-responsiveness). Most autistic people have a combination of both. Many autistic people are hypersensitive to bright lights and specific light wavelengths, such as those found in LED or fluorescent lighting. Other senses, such as specific noises, scents, textures, and tastes, can also be overpowering. This can lead to sensory avoidance, which is an attempt to escape from stimuli that most individuals can ignore with ease. Hyposensitive individuals may engage in sensory seeking to increase their environmental sensory input.

This can make everyday activities, such as going to the grocery store or getting a haircut, very difficult for people with autism as a result of sensory overload.

Autism can affect each of the seven senses in different ways. Here are some potential impacts on each sense:

Sight: Toddlers with autism may struggle with visual processing and interpreting what they see. They may also struggle with maintaining eye contact and be overly sensitive to light or visual stimulation. Visual processing difficulties are common in autistic people. This means they may have difficulty interpreting what they see or may see things differently than others. Some people with autism, for example, may see colors differently than others or have difficulty seeing objects in three dimensions. Bright colors may appeal to color-blind toddlers. Oversensitive toddlers may squint or appear uneasy under direct sunlight or glare.

Hearing: Toddlers with autism may struggle to absorb auditory information and be overly sensitive to sounds. They may also have difficulty communicating verbally and obeying verbal directions. Toddlers who are not very sensitive may crank up the music or speak too loudly. Toddlers who are overly sensitive may cover their ears to filter out loud noises.

Taste: Autistic toddlers may have issues with sensory processing, such as difficulty tolerating specific textures or flavors. They may also have a finite number of foods that they will consume. Some autistic people struggle with certain tastes and textures. Some people may be limited to a few foods, while others may be allergic to certain textures, such as slimy or crunchy dishes. Foods with strong flavors, such as onions and olives, may appeal to hyposensitive toddlers. Oversensitive toddlers may consume only certain textures of food. Mealtimes can be tough for families with autistic toddlers as a result of this.

Smell: Toddlers with autism may have a heightened sensitivity to certain smells or may be oversensitive to strong odors. They may also struggle to identify and name different smells. People with autism often have a heightened sense of smell. This can be both a blessing and a curse, as it can help people with autism identify certain smells more easily but can also make everyday smells overwhelming. Undersensitive toddlers might sniff everything. Oversensitive toddlers might complain about smells like deodorants or perfumes or smell things that no one else does.

Touch: Toddlers with autism may be oversensitive to certain textures or have difficulty tolerating certain types of touch. They may also have difficulty with tactile processing and struggle with tasks that require fine motor skills. People with autism often have either heightened or lowered sensitivities to touch. This means that they may either avoid being touched altogether or seek out deep pressure input such as squeezing or hugging. Undersensitive toddlers might seek out different textures or rub their arms and legs against things. Oversensitive toddlers might not like the sensation of labels on the inside of clothes or try to take their clothes off.

Temperature: Toddlers with autism may have a heightened sensitivity to temperature changes and may struggle with regulating their body temperature. They may also have difficulty tolerating certain clothing or materials. Undersensitive toddlers might want to wear warm clothes in the summer heat. Oversensitive toddlers might not feel the cold and want to wear shorts in the winter.

Proprioception: Toddlers with autism may have difficulty with proprioception, which is the sense of body awareness and position in space. This can affect their ability to coordinate their movements and may impact their gross motor skills. Undersensitive toddlers might have unstable balance. Oversensitive toddlers might have excellent balance.

The Benefits of Sensory Engagement for HFA Toddlers

Modification of the environment is the most accessible intervention for sensory processing difficulties. This involves assessing a toddler's sensory processing characteristics by considering their reactions to everyday experiences and modifying aspects of these experiences to counteract their hyper or hypo sensitivities. For example, a toddler who is overwhelmed by the noises and crowds in the high school hallway between classes may be encouraged to wear a cap and listen to music via their phones on AirPods or Bluetooth headphones during the transition between classes to moderate their visual and auditory stimulation.

Sensory play for toddlers is about hands-on activities that stimulate all or most of their senses. Sensory play focuses on activities that engage your toddler's senses, helping them develop language skills and motor skills. It also helps with cognitive growth, fosters social interactions, and encourages experimentation. This type of activity can benefit toddlers of all ages, but it's especially important for babies and young toddlers. Sensory play can help your toddler develop a wide range of skills in a fun, engaging way. And, given how many different sensory activities there are, it doesn't take a lot of effort to put one together for your toddler.

Sensory engagement can help HFA toddlers to self-regulate by providing them with the opportunity to explore different senses and textures. Sensory engagement can provide much-needed sensory input for some who may be hypersensitive or hyposensitive to certain stimuli. Tactile play specifically helps with fine motor skills, such as the ability to pick up small objects or to write. It also improves communication and language skills by teaching them how to describe the different objects they're interacting with or sensing. Sensory activities help to activate your toddler's problem-solving skills, which boosts overall cognitive development.

Sensory play can also address two other sensory systems that are often overlooked: our proprioceptive and vestibular systems. Proprioception and vestibular-based sensory play activities can help children develop their motor skills and coordination. It helps us understand the positions and motions of our various bodily components.

Improves Language Skills

The majority of babies can speak in simple words between the ages of 12 and 18 months, and by 2 years old, they may be speaking in complete sentences. Playing with their senses allows toddlers to explore and interact with their surroundings in meaningful ways, which can aid in language development.

Children are encouraged to recognize and express their emotions. Doing so allows them to learn from a wide range of experiences and environments. It is a starting point for assisting your toddler in using more extensive, descriptive language as they grow older.

Toddlers can learn new words and concepts fairly easily. Through sensory play, they encounter and describe new things and experiences, allowing for more growth and expression.

Sensory play, in general, helps toddlers learn and develop in exciting and engaging ways, which can also help with language development. It's a stepping stone to helping your toddler express how they feel, which will include bigger, more descriptive words as your toddler gets older.

Develops Fine and Gross Motor Skills

A toddler's development is dependent on the development of their fine and gross motor abilities, and sensory play is a simple way to accomplish this. While engaging in sensory play, your child will be exposed to a variety of objects with varying textures and forms. It allows your child to practice gripping and holding items while exploring and playing, assisting in the fun development of their motor skills.

During sensory play, larger muscles, such as those in the legs and torso, which are required for motions such as crawling, walking, and running, are used. It can also help kids improve gross motor abilities through activities like climbing, leaping, and tossing balls. Toddlers' fine and gross motor abilities are developed through sensory play. Fine motor abilities rely on smaller muscles, such as those in the hands and fingers. Gross motor abilities are required for activities such as crawling, walking, and running. Playdough and finger painting are two sensory play activities that may help with fine motor skill development. Sensory play is important for a child's development and should be encouraged.

It's a Calming Activity

Because sensory play is both engaging and soothing, it is ideal for a wide range of children with varying needs. It's a simple way to pique a child's interest and persuade them to participate in a beneficial activity if they're bored or sedentary. Giving hyperactive infants with short attention spans something to focus on is another method to help them.

These activities can help autistic children gain control of their environment while also assisting them in controlling their emotions and behavior. Sensory play benefits autistic toddlers because it provides them with a regulated, structured way to interact with their senses. Anxiety and tension can be reduced by regulating their emotional and sensory states. Sensory play can provide a sense of control and predictability for children with autism, who may suffer from sensory overload and unpredictable behavior.

Encourages Problem-Solving

A person with problem-solving skills can identify the source of a problem and find a solution. When engaged in sensory play, toddlers can use their senses to solve simple problems that are presented to them. This type of play encourages imagination, inventiveness, and self-assurance. It also promotes your toddler's autonomy because they will perceive their independence in problem-solving.

By handling items and materials, toddlers with autism can improve their cognitive and social abilities while learning about cause and effect. Sensory play improves concentration and attention in children because they must pay attention to the sensory input in order to engage with it. Ultimately, sensory play is a beneficial exercise that can help children with autism improve their problem-solving abilities and general development.

It's an Educational Opportunity

Sensory play allows youngsters to explore and discover new things while also improving their physical and cognitive skills. Toddlers can be introduced to a variety of textures and objects by introducing various sensory activities and toys. A natural sensory bin, which may be filled with natural materials such as leaves, twigs, flowers, and more, is one entertaining method to do this.

Toddlers may learn about the diverse forms and textures as they explore these objects, and parents can assist by labeling each item and encouraging children to explain its attributes. Through sensory play, children can obtain new knowledge and experiences while also improving their abilities to observe and explain their surroundings. Parents can assist children in their play by teaching them about the objects they are manipulating and encouraging them to define their characteristics.

Good for Information Retention

Information retention refers to our ability to

remember and use specific information stored in our long-term memory. Sensory play can help autistic toddlers process and organize information better, which will help their long-term memory grow. Although some people have naturally good memories, there are several ways to improve retention. Sensory play is especially beneficial for toddlers because it allows them to focus on an activity or job while also increasing their awareness of their surroundings. Toddlers can lay a solid foundation for their future memory by paying close attention and remembering what they are learning.

Through sensory play, toddlers can begin to refine their memory for new information and strengthen their information retention abilities. Toddlers with autism can become more aware of their surroundings and retain new information by engaging in activities that engage the senses and require concentration and focus. Furthermore, sensory play can help autistic toddlers feel calm and relaxed. This can improve learning and retention. Overall, sensory play is an important technique for helping them develop memory and knowledge retention.

Encourages Social Interaction

Toddlers should participate in as much social interaction as possible while they are still young, especially if they are the only child in the family. If your child participates in sensory activities with other toddlers, he or she has an excellent opportunity to form social relationships. Through sensory play, children can express their emotions and learn about the emotions of others. Sensory play is a fun way for toddlers to develop their social and cognitive skills. One of the primary benefits of sensory play is the development of social skills in toddlers.

Sensory play can help children develop their language skills by allowing them to express their emotions and learn new words. When children engage in sensory play, they are frequently required to interact with others and share materials. This helps them learn how to work together, express their needs and goals, and take turns. Children with strong social skills are better at following directions, staying focused, and resolving conflicts verbally. Through sensory play, children can investigate cause-and-effect relationships, make predictions, and test theories.

Can Help Improve Sensitivities

Hypersensitivity affects certain young toddlers and adults. This sensory processing disease makes the person extra sensitive to sensory stimuli such as light, sound, and touch. These sensations may not only be unpleasant, but they may also lead the individual to become distracted or angry. However, sensory play might aid children who are hypersensitive. It allows children to experiment with different sensations in a safe environment without being overstimulated. A fussy eater, for example, might play with the varied textures of meals they are wary of without feeling rushed.

Sensory play may benefit toddlers with autism because it can help them better understand and deal with sensory input. Sensory sensitivity describes how a person receives and responds to sensory information such as sights, sounds, and textures. Certain sensory domains in autistic people may be more or less sensitive, affecting how well they function and interact with their surroundings. Playing with soft materials or engaging in peaceful activities, for example, may benefit a child with autism who is overly sensitive to loud stimuli. On the other hand, playing with textured objects or participating in touch-based activities may be beneficial if they have a low threshold for touch.

20 Sensory Games and Activities to Play With Your Toddler

What you do to help your autistic toddler with sensory sensitivities depends on how your toddler reacts to sensory information. If your toddler is easily overwhelmed by sensory information, you could try the following:

- Have a "quiet space" your toddler can go to when they feel overwhelmed.

- Give your toddler extra time to take in what you're saying.

- Introduce your toddler to new places at quiet times, gradually increasing the amount of time they spend there in later visits.

- Let your toddler try earplugs or noise-canceling headphones to help with sound sensitivities.

If you're going somewhere, it's also a good idea to talk to people ahead of time about your toddler's needs; people may be able to change a few things to make things easier. For example, if you're planning a playdate for your child, you can request that it take place in a place where they feel at ease. You could look for theaters that offer sensory-friendly film screenings.

Here are 20 ideas for sensory games and activities that you can play with your high-functioning autistic (HFA) toddler:

1. Take walks outside together and discover all the sights, sounds, and fragrances that nature has to offer.

2. Go on a treasure hunt throughout your house or neighborhood, collecting various treasures as you go.

3. Make a "sensory bin" and fill it with various materials for your youngster to explore, such as grains, beans, pasta, playdough, and so on.

4. Make a mess together! Play with finger paints, mud, or whatever else gets your hands messy.

5. Cook or bake basic meals with your toddler, and allow them to help measure ingredients or stir the batter.

6. Enjoy all of your favorite foods during a picnic in your backyard or living room.

7. Read stories together and make up your own adventures with the characters.

8. Build towers out of blocks or Legos, or engage in any other form of construction game that your toddler enjoys.

9. Go on a "safari" around your house or neighborhood, looking for animals.

10. Make homemade pizzas, cookies, or whatever other foods your kid enjoys.

11. Play "Name That Tune" or build up your own dancing moves to favorite songs.

12. Take a bike ride or a walk to the park and enjoy the various playground equipment.

13. On a hot day, have a water war using squirt guns or water balloons.

14. In a tiny garden area, plant flowers or vegetables together.

15. Collect rocks, leaves, acorns, or any other natural thing to utilize in your art endeavors.

16. Perform simple scientific experiments with household ingredients such as baking soda and vinegar volcanoes.

17. Visit a zoo, aquarium, or museum to learn about the many animals and displays.

18. Play board or card games with your friends and take turns winning and losing.

19. Make up your own game rules for beloved games or build entirely new ones.

20.Simply spend time talking, laughing, and enjoying one another's company!

Chapter 9: Mastering Calmness

Emotional regulation is the ability to cope with situations that cause emotions like stress, anxiety, or frustration. Sometimes, people with autism have a harder time regulating their emotions. They may rely on unique self-soothing strategies to deal with intense emotions, and either seek out or avoid sensory stimuli like bright lights, loud sounds, and intense smells.

Autistic people who have trouble identifying their emotions, a condition known as alexithymia, are likely to have anxiety, depression, and problems with social communication, according to a new study. Alexithymia may also contribute to worsening mental health: People with severe alexithymia are more likely than those without to develop anxiety over time.

According to a University of Bristol study (Brysbaert, 2016) conducted by Dr. Geoff Bird in 2015, non-autistic adults with severe alexithymia are more likely to struggle with interpersonal interactions and are more likely to suffer from anxiety or despair. Approximately half of autistic persons have 'no language for feelings,' but little study has been conducted to determine how this impacts their mental health.

Why It's Hard for Children With Autism to Understand Emotions

One of the biggest challenges for people with autism is understanding emotions. They may have difficulty recognizing facial expressions or body language that indicate how someone is feeling. This can make it difficult for them to know how to respond in social situations.

Difficulty Expressing Emotions

Kids with autism may also have difficulty expressing their own emotions. They may not be able to use words to describe how they are feeling, or they may have trouble understanding the emotions of others. This can make it difficult for them to form relationships with others.

Sensitivity to Emotions

Some individuals with autism are very sensitive to the emotions of others. They may be able to pick up on subtle changes in facial expressions or body language that most people would miss. This can be both a blessing and a curse, as it can help them to understand the emotions of others but also make them very sensitive to emotional outbursts.

Emotional Outbursts

Children with autism may sometimes have emotional outbursts or tantrums. This can be due to frustration at not being able to express their emotions, or from feeling overwhelmed by the emotions of others. These outbursts can be very disruptive and cause problems in both personal and professional relationships.

Every person with autism manages their sensory input in a different way and their emotional regulation skills can vary. It's difficult to make any blanket statements on the signs of dysregulation. Dysregulation indicates that a person is having difficulty controlling their emotions. You may notice an increase in self-stimulatory activity, such as flapping, stimming, pacing, or rocking. If the person is able to express their emotions, asking how they are feeling is always a good sign. However, they may find it challenging to communicate their emotions in words.

It's also important to look at the environmental context to understand what's happening. Is it a new environment? Is it an environment they have been in before? What was their experience like the last time they were there? These questions can provide clues and guidance to help you support the autistic person.

Sometimes, an environment might be anxiety-provoking or full of a lot of sensory input. That can be both good and bad. Sometimes, the individual may be sensory-seeking and look for a lot of sensory stimulation from the environment. Other times, they may be sensory-avoidant and try to get away from stimuli. Watching the individual's behavior in the context of the environment can give you clues about what they are experiencing.

Why Emotional Self-Regulation Is
Important for HFA Toddlers

The ability to manage and modify one's behavior in response to emotions such as anxiety, frustration, or anger is referred to as emotional regulation. Teaching toddlers with autism how to regulate their emotions can help them develop socially and academically. Someone with good emotional regulation skills can recognize when they are experiencing strong emotions, consider the consequences of their actions, and take action toward their goals even when they are experiencing negative emotions.

On the other hand, a person who lacks emotional self-regulation may

- react more strongly to situations than their peers of the same age

- experience negative emotions for longer periods of time than their peers

- have a quick temper and display emotional outbursts

- experience mood swings

Developing emotional self-regulation skills is crucial for toddlers with autism as it allows them to recognize and understand their own emotions and the emotions of others, as well as the triggers that cause these emotions. It is important to teach toddlers when their emotions are becoming too intense and how they may impact their actions. Before teaching relaxation techniques, it is essential to help toddlers understand both positive and negative emotions.

Emotional self-regulation is especially important for autistic toddlers as it can help them cope with sensory overload, anxiety, and meltdowns. These skills can also improve their relationships with others and enable them to learn new skills and adapt to change more effectively. Teaching emotional self-regulation skills to toddlers can have a significant impact on their overall development and well-being.

Reduces anxiety

When we encounter toddlers who are difficult to control or who are having a breakdown or tantrum, we can see that their bodies are dysregulated. It could be because they're fatigued, overstimulated, frustrated, stressed, or a combination of other circumstances. Toddlers' ability to self-regulate is limited while they are very young. They begin to learn how to regulate their emotions by co-regulating with adults in their environment.

One part of co-regulation is modeling and prompting skills, which can assist a youngster in regaining control when they become dysregulated. This might be as simple as simulating deep breaths (not telling the child to take deep breaths). These tactics must be taught while the child's body and mind are calm and regulated. Have exercises, for example, to practice deep breathing when calm so that it is "easier" to use that ability during dysregulation.

What to Do When Your Toddler Has a Meltdown

Autistic toddlers frequently suffer with emotional dysregulation, making it challenging for them to manage their emotions in different contexts. This can result in behavioral difficulties like violent outbursts and meltdowns, as well as social anxiety and internalizing concerns. There are, however, ways that can help them enhance their emotional regulation skills as well as their overall well-being. Self-regulation exercises, which can help toddlers learn to control their emotions, are one approach to accomplish this. Another excellent strategy to improve their mental health and overall well-being is to teach relaxation techniques. Autistic toddlers can minimize the frequency of violent behavior and meltdowns, as well as social anxiety and internalizing concerns, by learning to regulate their emotions.

Understand what your toddler is feeling: Your child may be feeling overwhelmed, frustrated, or even scared. It's important to try to understand what your toddler feels and why. This can help you better respond to their needs.

Provide a safe space: Creating a safe space for your toddler will help them feel more comfortable and relaxed. This may include a quiet room where they can go to calm down, or a specific place in the house where they can go to feel safe.

Use calming activities: There are many activities that can help calm an autistic child. These may include deep breathing exercises, listening to relaxing music, or playing with a favorite toy.

Avoid overwhelming situations: If you know that your toddler is going to be in an overwhelming situation, such as a loud party or a crowded store, try to avoid it if possible. If you can't avoid it, try to prepare your toddler beforehand so that they know what to expect.

Don't punish your toddler: Punishing your toddler will only make them feel more anxious and stressed. Instead, try to provide positive reinforcement when they are able to calm themselves down.

Seek professional help: If you are struggling to calm your toddler, or if their anxiety is causing significant problems in their life, it may be time to seek professional help. A therapist or counselor who specializes in autism can provide you with additional tools and strategies for dealing with your toddler's anxiety.

Activities to Help Your Toddler Self-Regulate Their Emotions

Autistic toddlers, like any other toddler, experience a wide range of emotions, but they may require additional assistance in identifying, comprehending, and regulating these emotions. It is also critical to assist them in understanding and responding appropriately to the emotions of others. One important step in teaching autistic toddlers emotional awareness is to help them recognize and identify their own emotions as well as the emotions of others. Your toddler, for example, may be unaware that someone else is confused, sad, or angry, or they may mistakenly believe that someone else's negative emotions are directed at them. It is critical to help autistic toddlers understand the various emotions they may experience and how to appropriately respond to them.

You can use everyday interactions to help autistic toddlers learn about emotions. Here are some ideas for your toddler:

1) Label emotions as you come across them throughout the day. You can point out emotions when you're reading, watching TV, or visiting friends. Draw attention to your toddler's emotions. For example, "You're laughing. You must be having fun." Emphasize your own emotional responses. For example, "I am so happy! Give me a big smile!"

2) Assist your toddler in determining how their body feels when they are experiencing an emotion. "You seem nervous," for example. "Do you have a funny feeling in your tummy?" Draw a diagram of the body to show where people experience emotion, such as impaired

vision with cloudy eyes or a ringing in the ears with blocked ears.

3) Request that your toddler illustrate their feelings. Your child should be encouraged to play with emotions. Messy play, drawing or painting, puppet play, dancing, and music play are some play ideas to develop emotions in school-age toddlers.

4) With your toddler, engage in an emotion-based activity. With your toddler, choose an emotion, such as "sad," and simulate it. A straightforward guessing game can be made out of this activity.

The following emotional tools for your autistic toddler might be helpful:

- Use positive reinforcement, such as rewards, when your toddler displays positive emotional behaviors.

- Help your toddler understand what to expect each day by using a visual schedule.

- Social stories and comic strip conversations can help your toddler understand social situations. You can also try reading stories or comic strips about emotions.

- Practice deep breathing techniques, such as "blowing bubbles," to help your toddler relax.

- Use emotion cards featuring real or cartoon faces displaying various emotions to teach your toddler about emotions.

- Engage in sensory activities like playing with clay or sand to help your toddler regulate their emotions.

- Listening to soothing music together can also be a calming activity.

- Encourage your toddler to express their emotions through art, writing, or music.

- Introduce problem-solving and self-care skills as coping mechanisms to help your toddler manage their emotions.

Chapter 10: The Power of Movement

Toddlers with autism spectrum disorders (ASDs) frequently struggle to learn and use motor skills. The pool can be a good learning environment for these toddlers because it allows them to develop social, fitness, and aquatic skills. The principles of dynamic systems theory suggest that the interactions between the learner, task, and environment shape the development of movement patterns, which is consistent with a pool-based approach. The pool environment's unique features can help toddlers with ASD learn and practice new motor skills in a supportive and engaging environment.

Why Movement Is Helpful for HFA Toddlers

It helps them to explore their surroundings: Autistic toddlers may have difficulty investigating their surroundings and comprehending their place in the world. Movement allows them to interact with their surroundings, which can help them with this. Toddlers, for example, may crawl or walk around a room examining things, or they may use their hands and feet to feel objects.

It helps them to develop their coordination: Movement can also help autistic toddlers develop their coordination. This is because toddlers must move their bodies using their muscles and joints, which helps to develop coordination between these various parts of their bodies. They may not be aware of all of their physical components, but they can learn more about them as they move.

It helps them to develop their gross motor skills: Gross motor skills involve large movements that involve the use of our whole body, such as walking, running, and jumping. These skills are important for autistic toddlers to develop because they allow them to move around independently and join in group activities. Gross motor abilities are vital for autistic toddlers to learn and practice because they enable them to be more physically active and engage in a range of activities.

It helps them to develop their fine motor skills: Fine motor skills involve small movements of the hands and fingers, such as picking up a small object or writing with a pencil. These skills are essential for autistic toddlers to develop because they help them with everyday tasks like feeding and dressing themselves. Fine motor abilities are crucial for autistic toddlers to learn as they enable them to be more independent in their daily routines and activities.

It helps them to burn off excess energy: Many

autistic toddlers are hyperactive, which causes anxiety and overwhelm. Excess energy can be expelled through movement, allowing them to focus on other things and feel more at ease.

It helps them to socialize with other people: Exercise can help autistic children with socialization by providing a shared activity that they can all enjoy together. They may dance or play games together, for example, to help them participate in a pleasant and constructive way. Nonverbal communication, which is an important way of communication, can be aided by movement.

It Helps Them Focus: Autistic toddlers may struggle to focus on tasks or activities. Movement can improve concentration and focus by providing sensory input that anchors attention. This is especially beneficial for autistic toddlers who may struggle with attention and focus.

How HFA Children Use Physical Movement to Cope With Difficult Situations

Children with autism who engage in stimming behaviors (repetitive movements or behaviors) may have better control over negative emotions like anger, fear, and excitement. Stimming may assist them in relaxing and redirecting their attention to the stimming behavior, or it may cause a relaxing shift in their body. This is especially beneficial for autistic toddlers who may struggle with sensory overload. Stimming may also awaken "underactive" senses in people who are otherwise insensitive to sensory input in some cases. Broadly speaking, stimming behaviors can help autistic children and teenagers regulate their emotions and manage sensory information.

What Is Stimming?

Stimming is a repetitive behavior that is often seen in people with autism. It can take many different forms, but common examples include hand-flapping, rocking, spinning, and repetitive vocalizations. While stimming can be disruptive to those around the individual, it is often a way for the individual to cope with anxiety or sensory overload.

How Stimming Helps Toddlers With Autism

Stimming, or self-stimulatory behavior, is a common characteristic of autism. It can help toddlers with autism in a number of ways:

1) **It can provide a sense of comfort and calmness:** Stimming practices frequently have a repeated, rhythmic character that might be comforting to an autistic youngster. It can aid in the discharge of extra energy and stress in the youngster. Stimming gives the kid influence over their surroundings, which may

be highly beneficial in instances where they feel helpless. A toddler, for example, may rock back and forth or spin in circles to relax.

2) **It can serve as a form of communication:** Some autistic toddlers may use stimming to express their needs or emotions. A child, for example, may clap their hands or flap their arms to express excitement or happiness.

3) **It can help with sensory processing:** Sensory processing difficulties, such as over- or under-sensitivity to specific stimuli, may occur in autistic toddlers. Stimming practices can help these youngsters control and manage their sensory input. Stimming allows the kid to concentrate on a single job or activity, which can be beneficial when they are feeling overwhelmed by their environment. A youngster, for example, may hum their favorite song to assist them to focus on a certain activity or goal.

4) **It can help with social interactions:** Stimming behaviors can assist autistic toddlers in regulating their emotions and behavior in social situations. A child, for example, may use stimming to calm themselves down when they are overwhelmed by a social situation.

Overall, stimming can provide a sense of control and self-regulation for toddlers with autism, helping them cope with their environment and interact with others more effectively. However, as long as it does not harm your toddler or prevent them from learning, it is not necessarily a bad thing. Some stimming, such as extreme hand-biting, can be "harmful" to one's self. Stimming can also impair your toddler's ability to pay attention to the outside world, limiting their ability to learn and interact with others.

Common Types of Stimming

Although stimming varies greatly between people, it is common in autistic toddlers. Some toddlers, for example, stim more when they are worried or anxious. While some toddlers have mild hand mannerisms, others actively stim. Stimming can vary depending on the situation.

As mentioned above, there are many different types of stimming behavior. Some common examples include:

- hand-flapping

- rocking

- spinning

- repetitive vocalizations

However, stimming can also take less obvious forms, such as fidgeting, tapping, or staring at objects for long periods of time. Stimming might include

- hand and finger mannerisms, such as finger-flicking and hand-flapping

- odd bodily motions, such as swaying back and forth when seated or standing

- posturing, which is when you hold your hands or fingers out at an angle or arch your back while sitting

- looking at something sideways, seeing an object rotate, or fluttering fingers near the eyes, as examples of visual stimulation

- opening and shutting doors or flicking switches, as examples of repeated behavior

- chewing or mouthing objects

- listening to the same music or noise repeatedly

Why Do Autistic Children Stim?

Stims may help distract people with autism, relieve stress, or calm them down. While stims serve a purpose for the person doing the repetitive behavior, they can be distracting for other people who are around them.

There is no one definite answer to why autistic toddlers stim, as each child is unique and will have their own reasons for stimming. It would be wrong for us to generalize and put them all in one box. However, some common reasons include anxiety, sensory overload, and a need for self-regulation. Additionally, some toddlers may stim because it simply feels good or provides them with a sense of comfort.

While many people have a stim they use to self-regulate, it's not always obvious to others. As a result, people who stim may try not to stim in public and learn how to control the behavior. However, this is not possible for everyone who stims, since it's mostly unconscious behavior.

Autistic people experience significantly more severe stimming. This is because their perception of the environment is often more acute as a result of their enhanced senses. People with autism may jump up and down and flail their hands in excitement when they notice something interesting. It is not considered normal because so many people eventually learn to regulate these feelings and behaviors.

Many parents want to know how they can encourage their toddlers to stop stimming in order to help them fit in with their peers. Stimming, on the other hand, is quite common, if not socially acceptable. Instead of asking your toddler to stop stimming, try asking them why they are stimming.

Common Reasons for People to Stim

While we cannot generalize why people might stim, we can put it down to a few possibilities and try to understand what they may be dealing with.

Overstimulation: Stimming aids in the suppression

of excessive sensory input caused by overstimulation. In overwhelming situations that may cause them stress or anxiety, they may find ways to cope. This can be in loud or crowded spaces, or even if someone is asking them something, or paying too much attention to them.

Understimulation: Stimming offers additional sensory input if a location lacks sufficient sensory input—things to hear or see—or if a person is bored. An example of this type of stimming is clucking in a room that is too quiet.

Pain reduction: An autistic child's reaction may be to hurt themselves in another way to alleviate the pain if they fall or bump their arm. To alleviate other pain sensations, many kids bang their heads or bodies. Although it might seem counterproductive, medical experts think that this kind of stimming could release beta-endorphins that lessen pain or increase pleasure.

Management of emotions: Your toddler might start stimming when they experience sudden happiness or sadness. When they're angry or upset, they might flinch or start biting their nails.

Benefits of Stimming

Self-regulation: Whatever the situation, stimming allows us to stay grounded in the present moment and regulate our emotions. When someone with autism experiences a surge of emotions, that energy must be channeled somewhere. Stimming allows them to release that energy. It enables the individual to continue functioning within the confines of their current environment.

Mental health: When autistic people can self-regulate and process their emotions, they can improve their mental health. It may be a challenge if they have a stim that they consider embarrassing. They will usually try to redirect their stim into a more common movement.

How Can Parents Help Reduce Stimming?

There are a few things that parents can do to assist their autistic child who is stimming. It is critical to attempt to comprehend why the child is stimming and what purpose it serves for them. As a parent, you can provide opportunities for your toddlers to engage in positive outlets for their energy and emotions. This could be through physical activity or art projects. It is prudent to accept and understand the child's need to stim and to refrain from interfering with it unless it becomes disruptive or harmful.

Many autistic people believe they should be permitted to stim because it helps them. If your toddler is stimming a lot, it might be best for you to change their environment or help them manage their anxiety. Stimming can decrease as your toddler develops more skills and finds other ways to deal with sensitivity, understimulation, or anxiety.

Changing the environment

If the environment is too busy for your toddler, she may require a quiet place to go or only one item or activity to focus on at a time. Certain schools have sensory rooms for autistic toddlers who require more stimulation. There may be toys for toddlers to bounce or spin on, as well as materials for them to bury their hands in. If your toddler requires more stimulation, background music and a variety of toys and textures may be beneficial.

Working on anxiety

Determine your toddler's triggers and work to avoid or reduce them. This could include avoiding certain places or activities, taking sensory breaks, or using relaxing methods. Teach the child coping mechanisms to help them manage their anxiety and encourage healthy emotional expression. Consider seeking the help of a mental health professional to develop a personalized strategy to reduce your toddler's anxiety.

Tips for Developing Your Autistic Toddler's Motor Skills

The CDC recommends that toddlers engage in at least one hour of physical activity per day, but experts recommend starting low and working your way up. Shorter workout sessions spread out throughout the day are typically easier to maintain. Remember that the goal is to make exercise a regular and enjoyable part of your daily routine.

Remember that your toddler needs to develop some basic motor skills in order to participate in physical activities and sports successfully. Home practice of these skills may help your toddler's performance in physical education class, which increases the likelihood that your toddler enjoys other socially engaging physical activities such as playground games and recreational sports.

Concentrate on their strengths: Each child is unique and has their own set of strengths and weaknesses. When it comes to developing your toddler's motor skills, it is critical to concentrate on their strengths. It will help to boost their confidence and increase their chances of success.

Start with simple tasks: Try not to take on too much at once. Begin with simple tasks and gradually increase the level of difficulty as your toddler gains confidence and comfort.

Encourage them to practice: Perfect practice makes perfect, and this is especially true for improving motor abilities. Encourage your toddler to practice their abilities, whether it's writing their name, catching a ball, or riding a bike, on a regular basis. The more they practice, the better their motor skills will become.

Help them stay focused: Toddlers with autism may struggle to focus on a single task for a lengthy period of time. However, it is critical to assist toddlers in remaining concentrated in order to help them improve their motor abilities. One method is to break down jobs into smaller steps. If your toddler is learning to swim, for example, begin by having them enjoy splashing in the water for a few minutes at a time before advancing to learning how to kick or float.

Make it fun: Learning new motor skills can be intimidating for toddlers with autism; therefore, it is critical to make it enjoyable for them. One method is to incorporate games into the learning process. You could play "Simon Says" with your toddler by teaching them how to stomp their feet or kick a ball, for example. Games will not only make your toddler's learning experience more enjoyable, but it will also aid in their retention of information.

Reward them: It is critical to praise and reward your toddler when they demonstrate positive progress with their motor skills. This will stimulate and urge them to continue practicing. Anything from verbal praise to a small treat can be used as a reward.

Be a role model: As a parent, you are your toddler's most important role model. Show them how much you value and enjoy being active. If your town has recreational sports programs, you should contact them. Discuss your toddler's goals and plans. If your toddler has an Individualized Education Program (IEP), make sure to include physical education goals.

Movement-Based Activities to Try With Your Toddler

Here are three practical strategies commonly used in activity programs designed for youth who have autism:

1) **You need to be someone who understands:** It is important to educate yourself on programs regarding your toddler's abilities as well as the people whom you let them spend time with. Ideally, programs for physical activity should have facilitators who understand how to work with autistic toddlers as well as getting you as the parent involved. Even being able to find ways to create socialized peer interactions through physical activities is a good way to start.

2) **Routine:** Most of us require regularity, and many people on the spectrum appear to be no exception. Incorporate a regular and predictable framework into your and your toddler's physical activity schedule to ensure it is never skipped or forgotten.

3) **Get visual:** Many autistic persons are visual learners. Visual aids such as task cards, physical examples, and video modeling are frequently beneficial. You can even make a visual schedule to help you stick to the routine.

Now that you know how to approach these physical

activities, you can explore what your toddler likes doing. The following are possible fun activities for you to try out with your toddler and help them improve their motor skills:

- **Marching:** Marching is a simple gross motor practice that can help develop a variety of abilities. The task extends walking by requiring youngsters to imitate the steps. Encourage the youngster to start with leg motions in position, then go on to stepping and arm movements.
- **Play catch:** Playing catch is a great way to help your toddler develop their motor skills. It requires them to use their hands to catch and throw the ball, which can help to improve their coordination.
- **Ride a bike:** Riding a bike is another great way to help your toddler develop their motor skills. It requires them to use their legs and feet to pedal the bike, which can help to improve their balance and coordination.
- **Tunnel crawl:** Crawling through a tunnel can be a very enjoyable activity because it allows the child to use motor skills while also developing a sense of object permanence. Use peek-a-boo, hide-and-seek, and pretend play to incorporate social skills into the game. Arrange boxes to make a tunnel, or construct one out of chairs and blankets. The tunnel activity can be transformed into a variety of different things, such as a train or a campsite.
- **Play hopscotch:** Hopscotch is a great game that can help your toddler develop their motor

skills. They have to use their feet to hop on and off of the squares, which can help to improve their balance and coordination.

- **Play tag:** Playing tag is a great way to help your toddler develop their motor skills. They will need to use their legs and feet to run around, which can help to improve their stamina and coordination.
- **Draw with chalk:** Drawing with chalk is a great way to help your toddler develop their motor skills. This requires them to use their hands and fingers to hold the chalk and make shapes on the ground, which can help to improve their coordination.
- **Dance:** Dancing is a great way to help your toddler develop their motor skills. It requires them to use their whole body to move around, which can help to improve their coordination
- **Obstacle course:** Setting up an obstacle course is a great way to help your toddler develop their motor skills. This will get them to use their legs and feet to jump over obstacles, their arms to crawl under obstacles, and their whole body to balance on a beam.

Chapter 11: Sort Things Out

Children with autism spectrum disorder (ASD) frequently sort, stack, and arrange their toys because they find it reassuring. They prefer toys that can be categorized by color or pattern, such as dominoes, cards, and building blocks, because they find comfort in regularity and structure. Recent experimental research indicates that the categories formed by people with ASD may differ significantly from those formed by the majority of people (Mercado et al., 2020).

Autism and Sorting Skills

Sorting is a basic skill that helps toddlers understand and organize the world around them. It involves grouping objects based on characteristics such as size, shape, color, or other criteria. This skill is especially important for HFA toddlers, as it can help them improve their communication, socialization, and independent living skills.

Early intervention is crucial in helping HFA toddlers develop the skills they need to function in society. Sorting is a common activity for people with autism because it provides a sense of control and structure as well as sensory stimulation or relaxation. Some high-functioning autistic toddlers may use sorting as a way to focus their attention and reduce anxiety, while others use it to learn new skills such as categorizing and organizing information.

However, impaired sorting skills are a common symptom of autism, which means that HFA toddlers may have difficulty organizing objects based on certain characteristics. Fortunately, sorting skills can be improved with practice and repetition. By working on sorting activities with an HFA toddler, you can help them develop the skills they need to organize objects and understand their surroundings.

Sorting may be especially beneficial for HFA toddlers as it provides structure, sensory input, and a sense of control. This can be especially helpful for those who may have difficulty managing their emotions or processing sensory information. By incorporating sorting activities into their daily routine, your toddler can improve their skills and better cope with the challenges of autism.

Why HFA Toddlers Need to Sort and Categorize Things

When an autistic person organizes or arranges things, they are decreasing the signal-to-noise ratio, which means they are producing more signal and less noise by arranging their environment. This is a clever way to process information and can be especially useful for spotting patterns or flaws in chaotic data, which is important in programming and quality control applications.

HFA toddlers are at a stage in their development where they enjoy mastering things in their environment because it gives them a sense of control. Studies agree that it is best to approach toddlers with caution and understanding. Lining up items or arranging them in a specific order is a common behavior among autistic toddlers. Sorting and organizing skills are useful for toddlers to develop as they can improve numerical awareness, patterns, problem-solving skills, and object analysis.

Because HFA toddlers receive so much sensory input, they must filter and classify it to make sense of it. As a result, they often show a strong interest in sorting and categorizing items. This interest can be used to help them develop crucial abilities and improve their ability to process and understand information. By incorporating sorting activities into their daily routine, high-functioning autistic toddlers can improve their skills and better cope with the challenges of autism.

It helps them to make sense of the world: Autistic toddlers frequently fail to make sense of their surroundings. They can accomplish this by sorting and categorizing items. This assists them in organizing knowledge and understanding how many things are related to one another.

It helps them to communicate: Sorting and categorizing can also aid communication in autistic toddlers. For example, if an autistic child is shown a picture of a baseball, if they know it belongs in the category of "sports equipment," they may be able to identify it as a baseball. However, if they are unable to categorize it, it is possible that they will be unable to communicate what it is. Sorting and categorizing skills can thus assist autistic toddlers in understanding and communicating about the objects and concepts in their environment.

It helps them to focus: Autistic toddlers frequently struggle to focus on one thing at a time. Sorting and categorizing can assist them in focusing on a single task and blocking out distractions. This is especially useful when they are trying to learn new information or working on a project.

It helps them to stay calm: Sorting and categorizing can also assist autistic toddlers in remaining calm. This is due to the fact that it provides them with a sense of order and control. When everything is in its proper place, anxiety and stress levels can be reduced.

It helps them to interact with others: Sorting and categorizing can also aid in the interaction of HFA toddlers with others. This is because it gives them something to talk about and share with others, which can help them improve their social and communication skills. It can also help them understand other people's interests and find common ground, fostering friendships and positive social connections. HFA toddlers can improve their ability to communicate and interact with others by honing their sorting and categorizing skills, which can be especially beneficial for those who struggle with social interactions.

Sorting games are good for toddlers with autism for a few reasons:

1) **They promote organization and orderliness:** Toddlers are required to organize and classify items based on specific criteria, such as shape, color, or size. This helps them develop their ability to recognize patterns and order objects in a logical way, which can be beneficial for those who struggle with organization and attention to detail.

2) **They encourage problem-solving skills:** Toddlers must use their critical thinking and problem-solving skills to figure out how to classify and group items correctly. This can help them develop their ability to think logically and creatively, which can be beneficial for those who struggle with problem-solving tasks.

3) **They facilitate social interaction:** Many sorting games can be played with others, providing an opportunity for toddlers with autism to engage in social interaction and communication with their peers. This can help them develop their social skills and improve

their ability to communicate and interact with others.

4) **They provide a structured and predictable activity:** Sorting games provide a structured and predictable activity that can help toddlers with autism feel more comfortable and in control. This can help reduce anxiety and improve their ability to focus and engage in the activity.

Tips for Helping Your Toddler Develop Their Sorting Skills

Everyone wants to feel in control of their surroundings, and one way to do so is to establish order. As a result, many toddlers have an innate interest in sorting things and don't require much instruction. Meanwhile, some toddlers may require extra assistance getting started.

Sorting and categorizing activities can be an effective way to help high-functioning autistic toddlers improve their organization and problem-solving skills, as well as foster social interaction and provide a structured and predictable activity. These skills can be especially important for toddlers with autism, who may struggle with organization and attention to detail, problem-solving tasks, social interactions, and managing their emotions.

Here are some tips for helping high-functioning autistic toddlers develop their sorting skills:

- **Start with a small number of items:** It's important to start with a small number of items when introducing sorting to your child. This will help them feel less overwhelmed and more successful. Try starting with just a few items at first, and then gradually increase the number as your child becomes more comfortable with the task.

- **Use familiar items:** When introducing sorting to your child, it can be helpful to use familiar items that they are already familiar with. This could include their favorite toys or objects from around the house. This will help them make the connection between the objects and the task at hand.

- **Sort by one attribute at a time:** When teaching your child how to sort, it's important to focus on just one attribute at a time. For example, you could start by sorting by color, and then move on to sorting by shape or size. This will help your child understand the concept of sorting and make it less overwhelming.

- **Encourage your child to use their hands:** Sorting is a great opportunity for your child to use their hands and get some tactile input. Encourage them to pick up the objects and move them around.

- **Use visual aids:** When teaching autistic toddlers how to sort, visual aids can be extremely beneficial. You may help your child comprehend what they need to do by using drawings, diagrams, or even real-life objects. Having a visual picture of the task at hand will greatly assist your toddler in effectively completing the activity.

- **Use everyday objects:** You can also help your toddler sort by using everyday objects. You can, for example, organize clothes by color or silverware by type. You can even have your child assist you with sorting the recycling or putting goods away. The more opportunities for sorting your child has, the better!

- **Use sorting games:** Sorting games are an excellent approach to assist autistic toddlers practice their sorting skills. Sorting games are widely accessible online and in stores, so you should be able to find one that your toddler enjoys. Sorting games can help toddlers learn how to categorize objects based on color, shape, size, and other characteristics.

10 Sorting Games and Activities to Play With Your Autistic Toddler

1. Color sorting—provide your toddler with a variety of colored objects and have them sort them into different piles based on their color.

2. Shape sorting—provide your toddler with a variety of objects of different shapes and have them sort them into different piles based on their shape.

3. Size sorting—provide your toddler with a variety of objects of different sizes and have them sort them into different piles based on their size.

4. Texture sorting—provide your toddler with a variety of objects of different textures and have them sort them into different piles based on their texture.

5. Alphabetical sorting—provide your toddler with a variety of objects that have letters on them and have them sort them into different piles based on their first letter.

6. Number sorting—provide your toddler with a variety of objects that have numbers on them and have them sort them into different piles based on their number.

7. Matching—provide your toddler with a set of cards with matching pairs and have them match the pairs together.

8. Puzzle sorting—provide your toddler with a puzzle and have them sort the pieces into the correct places.

9. Clothing sorting—provide your toddler with a pile of clothing and have them sort them into different piles based on their type (e.g., socks, shirts, pants, etc.).

10. Food sorting—provide your toddler with a variety of different foods and have them sort them into different piles based on their type (e.g., fruits, vegetables, meats, etc.).

Chapter 12: Feed Your Child's Creative Side

Most people associate autism with rigid thinking, restricted interests, and a literal interpretation of speech and behavior. How could a person with these traits possibly be creative? Autistic toddlers have interesting outlooks on the world. The way they process information and see the world can be a bit different to how neurotypical people may see the world. This means that they have a knack for being creative in the most beautiful and curious ways.

HFA toddlers are often incredibly creative individuals. They tend to have unique perspectives and ways of thinking, which allows them to come up with creative solutions to problems and ideas. They may have a strong interest in a particular subject or activity, and this can lead to intense focus and dedication, which can result in impressive creations. For example, an HFA toddler may be interested in music and spend hours practicing and composing their own pieces. They may also excel in art or writing, using their unique way of thinking to create unique and imaginative pieces. Overall, HFA toddlers are often highly creative individuals who are able to take their interests and passions to new heights.

How Autism Affects Creativity

Autistic toddlers often have a unique perspective on the world, which can lead to creative ideas and artwork. However, some may have difficulty expressing their creativity or may be reluctant to try new things. Encouraging creativity in them can help them to express themselves and develop their own identity. Creative activities can also promote calmness and peace for them.

Autistic toddlers frequently have a strong interest in a specific subject or topic that they may obsess over. This acute attention can lead to more creativity as they are able to delve deeply into their passions. They may struggle with social contact and communication, making it difficult for them to convey their thoughts with others.

They can be more sensitive to sensory cues such as noises, scents, or textures, which can contribute to a higher awareness of their surroundings. However, it also implies that they are less likely to be affected by others and are more likely to generate creative ideas.

According to Cohen (2016), people on the autism spectrum are more creative and less prone to be limited by social standards than their neurotypical friends. When presented with a tool, they are more likely than their neurotypical counterparts to suggest other applications. They are also more likely to look outside the box when addressing problems.

Making art may be an unstructured or controlled activity that allows youngsters to develop their motor skills while drawing, painting, or learning an instrument. The sense of accomplishment that comes from creating an art creation is also an advantage that may boost confidence and self-esteem. For one thing, creativity may assist to promote resourcefulness, which is a crucial skill for self-sufficient individuals.

Although toddlers with autism spectrum disorders may struggle with social comprehension and awareness, many of them are extremely creative. Children on the autism spectrum can have a creative eye that sees possibilities everywhere, and if we do our bit to nurture that art, it can grow into a vital talent and interest. If given the opportunity, toddlers with ASD may create complicated and extremely inventive things.

Why Is It Important to Encourage Creativity in Autistic Toddlers?

It is important to encourage creativity in autistic toddlers for several reasons. First, creativity allows toddlers to express themselves and their unique perspectives in a way that may be more comfortable for them than verbal communication. This can help them to better connect with others and form meaningful relationships.

Additionally, engaging in creative activities can provide a sense of accomplishment and boost self-esteem, which is often a challenge for toddlers with autism. Creativity can also help to develop problem-solving skills and promote cognitive flexibility, which can be beneficial in many areas of life. Finally, encouraging creativity can provide an outlet for toddlers to manage their emotions and cope with stress in a healthy way. Overall, fostering creativity in them can have many positive effects and is an important aspect of their development and well-being.

It Helps Them Develop Important Skills: Encouraging creativity in autistic toddlers can help them develop important skills such as problem-solving, critical thinking, and communication. Additionally, creativity can also help them to express themselves and connect with others.

Sensory Stimulation: When autistic toddlers participate in the arts, they obtain a tactile sensation that may be extremely calming. Most toddlers with ASD may find playing with paint, crumpling papers, or arranging cubes to be both relaxing and sensory-stimulating. Trains may provide sensory stimulation for toddlers with ASD.

It Boosts Their Confidence: Allowing autistic toddlers to be creative can also boost their confidence. When toddlers feel like their ideas are valued and appreciated, it can help them feel good about themselves and their abilities. This helps them to express themselves and develop their own identity.

Developing Social Skills: When a toddler with (ASD) participates in creative activities such as art therapy or art courses, they may acquire social skills. Art therapy and art lessons create an atmosphere in which a kid with ASD may speak and learn while communicating and listening. The youngster will get more social skills as time goes forward.

It Increases Their Happiness: Creativity can also increase happiness in autistic toddlers. When toddlers are engaged in creative activities, they often feel a sense of joy and satisfaction. This can help to improve their overall mood and outlook on life by providing a much-needed outlet for emotions and help promote calmness and peace.

Creativity Helps to Express Emotions: Most autistic toddlers pay greater attention to details, and as a result, they may create wonderful art from their inventive minds. These youngsters create raw, passionate, and stunning art because they can think creatively beyond the box. Art may be used to relieve stress and communicate emotions that may otherwise go unspoken.

It Stimulates Their Imagination: Encouraging creativity in autistic toddlers can also stimulate their imagination. When toddlers are given the opportunity to be creative, they often come up with ideas that are outside the box. This can help to broaden their horizons and think about things in new and different ways.

It Teaches Them How to Be Persistent: Persistence is an important skill for all toddlers to learn, and creativity can help teach autistic toddlers how to be persistent. When toddlers are engaged in creative activities, they often have to try multiple times before they achieve the desired result. This helps them to learn that success is not always immediate, but that it is possible if they keep trying.

It promotes Well-being: When toddlers with autism do not have an effective means to communicate and have their views understood, they are more exposed to mental health difficulties. When youngsters are unable to express their feelings verbally, various behaviors may emerge to indicate that they require some attention. One method to help kids to express their feelings responsibly is via creativity.

It's Fun!: Last but not least, encouraging creativity in autistic toddlers is simply fun! When toddlers are given the opportunity to be creative, they often surprise us with their ideas and imagination. Seeing the world through their eyes can be a truly magical experience.

Tips for Promoting Your Toddler's Creativity

Encourage them to explore their interests: It is important to let your child explore their interests and allow them to find their own creative outlet. For example, if they are interested in painting, provide them with the supplies they need and encourage them to experiment. If they are interested in music, help them find an instrument they enjoy playing or sign them up for music lessons.

Provide structure: Some toddlers with autism thrive on structure and routine. If this is the case with your child, you can provide them with a structured environment that still allows for creative expression. For example, you could set up a weekly painting session where they have to complete a painting in one hour. Or you could have a daily music practice session where they have to play their instrument for 30 minutes.

Provide art supplies and materials that they are interested in: If your child is interested in cars, for example, provide them with crayons, paper, and coloring books featuring cars. If they're interested in animals, provide them with clay, paint, and brushes so they can sculpt or paint their favorite animals.

Provide opportunities to experiment: It is also important to encourage your child to try new things and step out of their comfort zone. This will help them to explore different interests and discover new talents. For example, you could sign them up for an art class or cooking class. Or you could take them to a museum or the theater.

Help them to find their own voice. Finally, it is important to help your child find their own voice and express themselves in their own unique way. This may involve trial and error, but it is important to let them experiment and find what works for them. For example, you could encourage them to keep a journal or diary where they can write down their thoughts and feelings. Or you could help them to start a blog or website where they can share their interests with the world.

Offer choices: Give your child choices in what they do and how they do it. This could include choices of activities, materials, or even just simple things like what color to use.

Respect their interests: Don't try to change or redirect your child's interests. Instead, respect their interests and encourage them to pursue them.

12 Activities to Help Nurture Your Toddler's Creativity

1. **Playdough:** Playdough/any kind of dough is a great way to encourage your child to use their imagination. They can make all sorts of shapes and figures with the dough, and they can even pretend to cook or bake with it.

2. **Blocks:** Blocks are another great way to encourage creativity. Your child can build towers, houses, bridges, or anything else they can think of.

3. **Painting:** Painting is a great activity for toddlers. They can experiment with different colors and textures, and they can create all sorts of masterpieces.

4. **Drawing:** Drawing is another great way for toddlers to express their creativity. They can draw pictures of their favorite things, people, or places.

5. **Collages:** Collages are a great way to help your child develop their fine motor skills. They can cut out pictures from magazines or newspapers and glue them onto paper to create a masterpiece.

6. **Music:** Music is a great way to encourage creativity. Your child can sing, dance, or even play an instrument.

7. **Make believe:** Make believe is a great way for toddlers to use their imaginations. They can pretend to be anything or anyone they want.

8. **Drama:** Drama is another great way to encourage your child's creativity. They can put on plays, skits, or puppet shows.

9. **Photography:** Photography is a great way to capture your child's imagination. They can take pictures of their favorite things, people, or places.

10. **Sculpting:** Sculpting is a great activity for toddlers. They can use clay, dough, or even

blocks to create all sorts of shapes and figures. Or build sand sculptures.

11. **Liquid soap foam or scented bubbles:** These materials can give a multi-sensory experience that engages several senses at once. Soft, fluffy foam that may be readily sculpted and molded, and it can provide children with an unusual sensory experience. Scented bubbles add a sensory aspect to play because children can smell and see the bubbles as they float through the air.

12. **Practice "joint attention":** Directing attention from one thing to another. This can help expose children to stimuli and ideas, sparking their creativity. Building using blocks, Legos, or other materials can be a fun approach to improve joint attention and foster creativity. You can direct your toddler's attention to various forms, sizes, and colors, as well as encourage them to experiment with various structures and patterns.

Conclusion

You are now armed with an arsenal of skills, tips, and activities to get involved with your HFA child. Understanding their diagnosis, symptoms, and even the myths the world has about them allows you to help them navigate the world in a safer way. It also allows you to have peace of mind knowing that you can tackle most problems that may come your way, including setting the record straight.

A happier, less stressful, and less anxiety-filled life is ahead of you. You now have so many ways to help nurture your child's strengths and develop your child's weaknesses. This includes the nine strategies for developing their communication and socialization skills. Weak points or missed milestones are no longer worries, because you understand them, and now you know how to help your child gain the skills they need to survive in this society.

You now know where to go and how to ask for help: From finding sanctuary in the community to considering professionals and facilitators; even getting teachers and schools involved. It truly takes a village in this case. You also know what you are capable of, and you know what your child is capable of. By learning your limitations, you know how much you can do on your own and what you can include in your daily routine.

Start with communicating with your child in a way

that they are comfortable with and then learning how they want to play with you and others. By bonding with your child in so many new ways, you allow them to socialize and use all their senses in a way that helps them be stimulated in the correct ways. When they are overstimulated, you now know calming techniques. Lastly, you know how to promote movement, sorting skills, and creativity in your child, allowing them to grow and develop in a healthy and safe environment.

You and your family will be the next success story other families read about, and it may be a way for others to get the help they need, just like you got the help you needed right here. Try out all the strategies you have learned about and put them into action. But remember to be patient, not only with your toddler, but with yourself as well. Parenting is a process, and it takes time.

If you enjoyed this book, please be so kind as to leave a review. Thank you.

Glossary

All definitions were adapted from the *Merriam-Webster* dictionary.

Alexithymia: Difficulty identifying and expressing one's own and others' emotions, frequently accompanied by a restricted imagination and a focus on practical things. Alexithymia can be linked to a variety of physical illnesses or personality qualities, and it can have an impact on interpersonal interactions and communication. It could necessitate therapy or management.

Anxiety: A group of negative emotions such as worry, fear, and unease that may come with physical symptoms like shortness of breath, chest pain, or stomach pain.

Applied Behavioral Analysis (ABA): A scientific discipline that uses principles of learning and behavior to address socially significant issues. It involves measuring observed behavior and analyzing the relationship between that behavior and environmental events that precede or follow it.

Assistive Technology: Any equipment or item used to improve, maintain, or increase the functional capabilities of individuals with disabilities.

Asperger's Syndrome (AS): A former diagnostic label used to describe a person with an ASD who did not have a language delay or any intellectual disability.

Attention: The mental process of selectively focusing on one thing while ignoring others.

Attention Deficit Hyperactivity Disorder (ADHD): A neurological condition with chronic core symptoms such as distractibility, disorganized thinking, poor impulse control, mood shifts, forgetfulness, and hyperactivity. These symptoms can vary in different situations and at different times. Common secondary symptoms include emotional and perceptual immaturity, poor social skills, disruptive behaviors, and academic problems. It is believed to affect 3–5% of the population.

Autism: A complex neurological and developmental disorder that impacts communication and social interaction. Symptoms typically appear in early childhood and may include repetitive behaviors, difficulty with communication and social interaction, and sensitivity to sensory stimuli.

Autistic Disorder: A former diagnostic label used to describe a person with an ASD.

Autistic Savant: An individual with autism who displays exceptional skill in a specific field (e.g., music, math).

Autism Spectrum Disorder: A developmental disability that refers to individuals who have difficulties with social communication/interaction and exhibit restrictive and/or repetitive patterns of behavior.

Co-existing Disorders: In addition to cognitive impairments, individuals with ASD often experience multiple mental health conditions at the same time, such as impulse-control disorders, psychoses, obsessive-compulsive disorder, seizures, mood and anxiety disorders, and developmental delays. These are also referred to as "comorbid disorders," "differential diagnosis," or "dual diagnosis."

Cognition: The mental process of perceiving, reasoning, problem solving, and remembering.

Cognitive: The ability to carry out daily tasks in a functional manner, including the ability to remember short and long term events, sequence activities, reasoning, thinking logically and safely, and categorizing.

Cognitive Behavioral Therapy: A treatment that combines behavior therapy with cognitive therapy and aims to reduce habitual reactions to challenging situations. CBT helps individuals learn how certain ways of thinking may contribute to negative emotions and behaviors. Research has shown that CBT may be effective for some people with HFA. This treatment is provided by a trained psychologist and may be used with toddlers, adolescents, or adults who are able to speak.

Comorbidity: Conditions that coexist with, but are usually unrelated to, another medical disease. When a person has two or more distinct conditions at the same time, this is referred to as co-morbidity. A person may have both Fragile X syndrome and autism, or both an anxiety disorder and autism.

Communication Disorder: Any impediment to a person's understanding or expression of ideas, experiences, knowledge, or feelings.

Compulsion: An irresistible recurring inclination or desire to execute an act, generally repetitive or obsessive in nature, that a person feels compelled to perform and finds difficult to resist or control. Compulsions can interfere with a person's everyday life and cause distress or worry as a sign of mental health issues such as obsessive-compulsive disorder (OCD) or Tourette's syndrome. Therapy and medicine may be used in treatment.

Daily Schedule: A daily schedule is intended to give a person's day predictability and organization. A daily plan can also be utilized to enhance "on task" (engaged) behavior while decreasing inappropriate behavior. A daily plan, in general, assists a person in properly organizing and managing their time.

Data Collection: Data collection and analysis are required for making informed decisions about a person's behavior or academic performance. Methods for gathering data include parent interviews, grading papers, and curriculum-based evaluations. It is critical to have a well-organized and methodical approach to data gathering to ensure the authenticity of the data.

Developmental: Referring to the process of a person's growth, maturation, or progressive change as they age.

Developmental Language Disorder: A developmental language disorder is a condition that causes children to struggle with language development. These challenges may include difficulties expressing thoughts or interpreting written or spoken language. Developmental language disorders are frequently diagnosed in childhood and can severely impair a child's capacity to speak and learn.

Developmental Disability: A developmental disability is a condition that affects a person's physical, cognitive, or social development and is typically apparent throughout childhood or infancy. Autism, cerebral palsy, intellectual disability, blindness, and fragile X syndrome are examples of these disabilities. Delays or restrictions in learning, language, communication, cognition, behavior, sociability, or mobility can result from developmental disabilities. These illnesses can have a major influence on a person's everyday life and may necessitate continuing care and treatment.

Diagnostic and Statistical Manual (DSM-5): The official system for classification of psychological and psychiatric disorders, prepared by and published by the American Psychiatric Association. The number at the end, in this case '5', indicates the version of the DSM released.

Early Intensive Behavioral Intervention (EIBI): EIBI is a treatment strategy that combines applied behavioral analysis (ABA) concepts to assist very young children with autism spectrum disorder. EIBI programs can be delivered at a clinic, at home, or in a school setting, and can include scheduled activities as well as one-on-one training. It seeks to enhance outcomes for children with ASD by assisting them in functioning as independently as feasible.

Echolalia: Repeating previously heard words or phrases. The echoing can happen shortly after hearing the word or phrase, or it can happen decades afterwards. Delayed echolalia can occur days or weeks after the word or phrase is heard.

Environmental Engineering: Environmental engineering is a field that focuses on preserving and improving the natural environment. It also involves understanding the impact of the physical environment on human behavior and learning. Environmental engineers may design physical spaces to encourage positive behaviors and improve learning and performance.

Executive Functioning: The mental processes and cognitive abilities involved in task planning, organization, and execution are referred to as executive functioning. Working memory, impulse control, and reasoning are among the skills required for goal-directed action. Executive functioning abilities are required for time management, information recall, activity planning, and problem solving. These abilities, known as "executive functions," are critical for academic, occupational, and personal success. Executive functioning can be influenced by a number of factors, such as age, stress, and mental health disorders, and it can be improved with certain therapies, such as counseling or medication.

Functional Analysis: A functional analysis is a method for determining the underlying causes of a behavior. It entails systematically modifying the behavior's antecedents and consequences in order to determine which factors are driving the behavior. A functional analysis is commonly used in the context of behavior modification, with the goal of changing or eliminating problematic behaviors. Experiments or other systematic methods may be used to confirm the causes of the behavior and develop an appropriate intervention plan.

Generalization: Generalization is the act or process of formulating broad claims, rules, principles, or propositions based on limited or specialized observations or experiences. It can also refer to a learned response to a similar but not identical stimulus to the initial stimulus. A person who has learned to associate a specific sound with a specific event, for example, may react to similar noises, such as a doorbell or ringing phone.

High-Functioning Autism (HFA): High-functioning autism (HFA) is a type of autism spectrum disorder (ASD) in which people have difficulties with social interaction, communication, and repetitive behaviors but can perform many daily tasks and frequently have an above-average IQ. People with HFA may have milder ASD symptoms and go undiagnosed until later in childhood or even adulthood. They may require assistance and accommodations in certain areas, such as social relationships or communication, but they are often able to function independently and participate in traditional school or job settings. Although it is no longer used in the DSM-5 diagnostic manual for ASD.

Hyperactive: Influenced by or exhibiting hyperactivity; in general being more active than is usual or desired.

Hypersensitive: A state of being overly or unusually sensitive to anything is referred to as hypersensitivity. This can relate to physical or emotional sensitivity, such as being quickly irritated or upset by specific stimuli. Hypersensitivity to some stimuli might be a natural reaction, but it can also be an indication of a medical issue. Hypersensitivity can create undesirable responses or symptoms in some circumstances, which may necessitate therapy or management.

Individualized Educational Program (IEP): A written plan defining the educational goals, resources, and accommodations required to support a student with special education needs is known as an Individualized Educational Program (IEP). An IEP is created by a team of professionals, including teachers, parents, and other specialists, and is tailored to the student's specific needs and skills. It is regularly reviewed and revised to ensure that the student is making progress and receiving the necessary help to succeed in school.

Intellectual disability: A condition with severe limitations in cognitive functioning and adaptive behavior, impairing a person's ability to learn, communicate, and function independently. It may be present from birth or caused by an injury, disease, or other factor. It is diagnosed based on cognitive and adaptive behavior assessments and may require ongoing support and accommodations.

Integration: In the context of education, integration refers to the inclusion of children with disabilities in regular classrooms and school activities, as well as the participation of different communities in all sectors of society. Integration can entail a variety of efforts and techniques, such as making accommodations and providing support to students with disabilities, developing cultural sensitivity and knowledge, and advocating for equitable access and opportunity for all members of a community.

IQ (Intelligence Quotient): An obsolete word referring to a person's cognitive ability or level of intellect as determined by a standardized exam based on a cognitive aptitude measure. It measures a person's ability to think abstractly, solve problems, and learn new information and is commonly expressed as a score on a scale of 100. Although IQ is used to predict academic and intellectual achievement, it is not the only element that predicts success or abilities.

Joint attention: The ability to share the experience of paying attention to an object or activity with another person. Following another person's gaze, directing their attention toward an object of interest, or switching back and forth between an object and another person while engaging in a shared activity are all examples of this. Joint attention is a vital social ability for communication and learning that is commonly formed in the first years of childhood. Children with developmental delays or impairments may struggle with joint attention and may require assistance and intervention to enhance this skill.

Language: The ability to convert an idea into a grammatical sequence of words (verbal or written mode). This includes the ability to employ a learned skill in both a receptive and expressive manner.

Low-Functioning Autism (LFA): is a type of autism spectrum disorder (ASD) that is distinguished by severe limitations in social interaction, communication, and repetitive activities, as well as significant intellectual and developmental disabilities. People with LFA may struggle with many daily tasks and may require extensive support and assistance in order to participate in school, work, and other activities. Although the term "classic autism" is commonly used to describe LFA, it is no longer used in the DSM-5 diagnostic criteria for ASD.

Mobility: The ability to physically move about and engage in work or exercise.

Motor Planning: Motor planning is the process of arranging and coordinating the motions and activities required to perform a job or activity. To organize, sequence, and execute motions in a smooth and efficient manner, sensory, cognitive, and motor skills must be integrated. Motor planning is a necessary skill for everyday tasks such as dressing, eating, and bathing, as well as more complex ones such as sports and other physical activities. Motor planning may be difficult for children with developmental delays or impairments, and they may require assistance and intervention to improve this ability.

Natural Environment: The home and other community settings where toddlers and families regularly participate in activities are considered the natural environment. Early intervention services must be given in natural settings to the greatest degree possible to meet the needs of the child and family.

Neurodivergent: Individuals who are neurodivergent have developmental abnormalities or other neurological differences that affect their cognition, behavior, and communication. Individuals who are neurodivergent may have autism spectrum disorder, attention deficit hyperactivity disorder (ADHD), dyslexia, or other problems that alter how their brains process and interpret information. The term neurodivergent is frequently used in contrast to neurotypical individuals. Individuals who are neurodivergent may require assistance and accommodations in order to fully participate in school, job, and other activities.

Neurotypical: Refers to a person who has usual neurological development and is not impacted by a developmental disorder, specifically autism spectrum disorder. Neurotypical people may not have the same experiences or obstacles as people with developmental disorders, and their cognitive, social, and emotional skills and capacities may differ. Neurotypical is frequently used in contrast to neurodiverse, which refers to people with developmental problems or other neurological differences.

Nonverbal Communication: Nonverbal communication refers to methods of communication that do not involve the use of words. Body language, facial expressions, gestures, eye contact, and other types of physical communication are examples of this. Nonverbal communication is an important part of human connection since it can transmit a variety of emotions and intentions. It can also help with the interpretation and comprehension of verbal communication.

Picture Exchange Communication System (PECS): A form of alternative communication in which image symbols are used to facilitate conversation. It is commonly taught in six stages, beginning with the exchange of a picture symbol for a desired item and proceeding to the use of image symbols to create whole phrases, initiate dialogue, and respond directly to direct queries. PECS is frequently used with people who have trouble communicating verbally, such as those with autism spectrum disorder or other developmental impairments, and it can be a useful tool for enabling communication and increasing social interaction.

Perseveration: Repeating a movement, task, or thought with a compulsive quality. It can be normal or a symptom of medical conditions like OCD or brain injury, and may require treatment.

Positive Behavior Supports: Strategies and practices that assist people in developing and engaging in adaptive and socially desirable behaviors while decreasing destructive or stigmatizing responses.

Receptive Language: The capacity to comprehend spoken language.

Regulation: Controlling or governing something, typically by the application of rules or laws. Regulation in biology refers to the process of maintaining a steady internal environment in the body, such as blood pressure or body temperature. Regulation is defined in psychology as the ability to control one's thoughts, emotions, and behaviors, particularly in reaction to internal or external stimuli. Regulation is a crucial part of both mental and physical health that can be aided by a variety of tactics and interventions.

Self-Injurious Behavior (SIB): Causing harm to your own body, e.g., cutting or burning oneself.

Sensory Integration (SI): This is the process through which the brain processes sensory stimuli or sensations from the body and then converts that information into particular, planned, and coordinated motor movement. The brain's structuring and interpretation of sensory data from the body and environment in order to create adaptive responses.

Sensorimotor: Concerning the interaction of the senses (such as sight, touch, and hearing) with movement. Sensorimotor activity, as opposed to automatic operations like respiration and circulation, involves voluntary movements that are directed by the brain. It is a critical stage of development that can be influenced by neurological problems or accidents.

Sensory Processing: Sensory processing is the process through which the brain evaluates and organizes sensory input in order to generate meaningful and adaptive responses. It can be evaluated for and diagnosed as "Sensory Processing Disorder," which affects people other than those with ASD. The sensory function of children can also be monitored in order to better understand their sensory processing ability.

Stereotyped behaviors: Repetitive actions that are common in people with developmental problems like autism. These behaviors can vary in frequency and intensity and may involve a specific body region or activity. They can be used as a coping strategy or a means of communication, but they can also disrupt daily functioning and social interactions. Behavioral stereotypes may necessitate intervention or management.

Stim: Behaviors that engage the senses are common among autistic people and may serve as a technique to manage emotions or concentration. Stimming habits can be characterized by repetitive motions or sensory input. They may be inappropriate or disruptive in social situations, but they can also act as a coping mechanism.

Visual Aids: Objects or media that aid in the visual transmission of information and are used to augment or improve oral or written presentations. Visual aids can help to clarify concepts, demonstrate examples, emphasize key points, and engage the audience. They are effective teaching and learning tools that may be used in a variety of circumstances.

References

15 fun outdoor activities for children with autism. (2016, July 28). Therapy Source. https://txsource.com/2016/07/28/15-fun-outdoor-activities-for-children-with-autism/

A quote from the way I see it. (n.d.). Www.goodreads.com. Retrieved December 9, 2022, from https://www.goodreads.com/quotes/386850-what-would-happen-if-the-autism-gene-was-eliminated-from

Administrator. (2019, April 16). *Art & autism: The importance of creativity for children on the spectrum.* The Place for Children with Autism. https://theplaceforchildrenwithautism.com/autism-blog/art-autism-the-importance-of-creativity-for-children-on-the-spectrum#:~:text=Children%20have%20an%20inherent%20sense

Allen, S. (2016, April 5). *Color sorting activity.* The Autism Helper. https://theautismhelper.com/color-sorting/

Allen, S. (2017, June 21). *Teaching categorization skills.* The Autism Helper. https://theautismhelper.com/teaching-categorization-skills/

Alokla, S. (2018). *Non-Verbal communication skills of children with autism spectrum disorder.* https://scholarworks.lib.csusb.edu/cgi/viewcontent.cgi?article=1796&context=etd

Amanda Augustine. (2022, October 12). *Importance of play based learning for children with autism.* EAS. https://earlyautismservices.in/importance-of-play-based-learning-for-children-with-autism/

Angulo, J. (2021, May 3). *LibGuides: LIS 511- autism spectrum disorder in children: Communication is key.* Liupalmer.libguides.com. https://liupalmer.libguides.com/c.php?g=1141657&p=8354153

Aruma. (2015, December 4). *Myths about autism spectrum disorder | aruma.* Aruma Disability Services. https://www.aruma.com.au/about-us/blog/myths-about-autism-spectrum-disorder/

Autism Awareness Australia. (2019, July 11). *Why we should stop using the term "high functioning autism."* Www.autismawareness.com.au. https://www.autismawareness.com.au/aupdate/why-we-should-stop-using-the-term-high-functioning-autism

Autism communication strategies that work. (2022). The

Spectrum. https://thespectrum.org.au/autism-

strategy/autism-strategy-communication/

Autism social interaction strategies. (n.d.). The Spectrum.

https://thespectrum.org.au/autism-strategy/social-

interaction/

Autism Speaks. (2013). *Sensory issues.* Autism Speaks.

https://www.autismspeaks.org/sensory-issues

Autism Speaks. (2019a). *Recreation.* Autism Speaks.

https://www.autismspeaks.org/activites-children-

autism

Autism Speaks. (2019b). *Social skills and autism | autism

speaks.* Autism Speaks.

https://www.autismspeaks.org/social-skills-and-

autism

Autistic children struggle with hidden emotions - ARU. (2021,

October 7). Aru.ac.uk.

https://aru.ac.uk/news/autistic-children-struggle-

with-hidden-emotions

Autistica. (2019, April 9). *Myths and causes - autism |

autistica.* Autistica.

https://www.autistica.org.uk/what-is-autism/autism-

myths-and-causes

Badiah, L. I. (2018). The importance of social skills for autism.

Proceedings of the 2nd INDOEDUC4ALL -

Indonesian Education for All (INDOEDUC 2018).

https://doi.org/10.2991/indoeduc-18.2018.7

Barloso, K. (2019, July 29). *Autism social skills: How to enhance social interaction - autism parenting magazine.* Autism Parenting Magazine.

https://www.autismparentingmagazine.com/autism-social-skills/

Bauminger, N., Solomon, M., Aviezer, A., Heung, K., Brown, J., & Rogers, S. J. (2007). Friendship in High-functioning Children with Autism Spectrum Disorder: Mixed and Non-mixed Dyads. *Journal of Autism and Developmental Disorders, 38*(7), 1211–1229.

https://doi.org/10.1007/s10803-007-0501-2

Bennie, M. (2020, October 7). *The importance of play for children with ASD.* Autism Awareness.

https://autismawarenesscentre.com/the-importance-of-play-for-children-with-asd/

Bernier, R. (2016, May 31). *Through play, children with autism can hone thinking skills.* Spectrum | Autism Research News.

https://www.spectrumnews.org/opinion/viewpoint/through-play-children-with-autism-can-hone-thinking-skills/Brysbaert, M. (2016). Proceedings of the experimental psychology society 2016. Quarterly Journal of Experimental Psychology, 69(12), 2487–

2502.

https://doi.org/10.1080/17470218.2016.1237416

Bogart, L. (2019, March 4). *How to help your child with autism understand their emotions*. Hopebridge Autism Therapy Center. https://www.hopebridge.com/blog/understand-emotions-child-autism/

Brignell, A., Chenausky, K. V., Song, H., Zhu, J., Suo, C., & Morgan, A. T. (2018). Communication interventions for autism spectrum disorder in minimally verbal children. *Cochrane Database of Systematic Reviews, 11*. https://doi.org/10.1002/14651858.cd012324.pub2

Brysbaert, M. (2016). Proceedings of the experimental psychology society 2016. *Quarterly Journal of Experimental Psychology, 69*(12), 2487–2502. https://doi.org/10.1080/17470218.2016.1237416

Busti Ceccarelli, S., Ferrante, C., Gazzola, E., Marzocchi, G. M., Nobile, M., Molteni, M., & Crippa, A. (2020). Fundamental Motor Skills Intervention for Children with Autism Spectrum Disorder: A 10-Year Narrative Review. *Children, 7*(11), 250. https://doi.org/10.3390/children7110250

CDC. (2022, March 31). *Autism and developmental disabilities monitoring (ADDM) network | CDC*. Centers for Disease Control and Prevention.

https://www.cdc.gov/ncbddd/autism/addm.html#:~:
text=What%20We

Cleveland Clinic Pediatrics. (2022, March 18). *What is sensory
play? The benefits for your child and sensory play
ideas.* Cleveland Clinic.
https://health.clevelandclinic.org/benefits-of-
sensory-play-
ideas/#:~:text=Sensory%20play%20focuses%20on%
20activities

Cohen, B. (2016, December 16). *Autism and creativity |
psychology today canada.*
Www.psychologytoday.com.
https://www.psychologytoday.com/ca/blog/mom-
am-i-disabled/201612/autism-and-creativity

Communication in children with high-functioning autism.
(n.d.). Www.hanen.org. Retrieved December 7, 2022,
from http://www.hanen.org/About-Us/What-We-
Do/High-Functioning-
Autism.aspx#:~:text=But%20for%20children%20wit
h%20high

Corona, L. (2019). *Teaching communication skills: A toolkit
for educators.*
https://vkc.vumc.org/assets/files/resources/teach-
com-skills.pdf

Dattaro, L. (2020, November 12). *Difficulty identifying emotions linked to poor mental health in autistic people.* Spectrum | Autism Research News. https://www.spectrumnews.org/news/difficulty-identifying-emotions-linked-to-poor-mental-health-in-autistic-people/

Day, N. (2018, February 14). *120 emotional self-regulation ideas for kids - autism & ADHD resources.* Raising an Extraordinary Person. https://hes-extraordinary.com/self-regulation-strategies

de Fina, C., & Anderson, A. A. (2017, July 7). *Play and children with autism spectrum disorder.* Raising Children Network. https://raisingchildren.net.au/autism/school-play-work/play-learning/play-asd

Disabled Living. (2019, May 24). *6 fun activities to help you bond with your autistic child.* Disabled Living. https://www.disabledliving.co.uk/blog/activities-to-help-you-bond-with-your-autistic-child/

Draycot, C. (2018, June 16). *Using art and creativity to engage an autistic child in the classroom.* The Art of Autism. https://the-art-of-autism.com/educating-autism-art-and-creativity-to-engage-an-autistic-child-in-the-classroom/

Easy Daisies. (2016, April). *Autism: 5 things you should know about children with ASD*. Easy Daysies. https://www.easydaysies.com/blogs/blog/autism-5-things-you-should-know-about-children-with-asd

Encouraging Pretend Play in Children with Autism or Social Communication Difficulties. (n.d.). Www.hanen.org. http://www.hanen.org/Helpful-Info/Articles/Encouraging-Pretend-Play-in-Children-with-Autism.aspx

Expert Q&A: Understanding emotional regulation in autism. (2022, May 19). Autism Speaks. https://www.autismspeaks.org/blog/expert-qa-understanding-emotional-regulation-autism

Flint, C. (2015, September 8). *Why is sorting a great way to build skills for individuals with autism?* InfiniTeach. https://www.infiniteach.com/blog/sort-activity-children-with-autism/

Goally. (2022a, February 24). *Tips for parenting a child with high functioning autism*. Goally. https://getgoally.com/blog/tips-for-parenting-a-child-with-high-functioning-autism/

Goally. (2022b, August 3). Why is play difficult for children with autism spectrum disorders? *Goally*. https://getgoally.com/blog/autism-play-difficult/

Granato, G., Borghi, A. M., Mattera, A., & Baldassarre, G. (2022). A computational model of inner speech supporting flexible goal-directed behaviour in autism. *Scientific Reports, 12*(1), 14198–14198. https://doi.org/10.1038/s41598-022-18445-9

GriffinOT. (2019, December 24). *ASD and Sensory Processing Disorder - A Brief Introduction.* GriffinOT. https://www.griffinot.com/asd-and-sensory-processing-disorder/

Hagan, E. (2016, December 18). *Autism and creativity | psychology today south africa.* Www.psychologytoday.com. https://www.psychologytoday.com/za/blog/mom-am-i-disabled/201612/autism-and-creativity

Healis Autism Centre. (2021a, January 26). *Importance of play for children with autism.* Healis Autism Centre; Healis Autism Centre. https://www.healisautism.com/post/importance-play-children-autism

Healis Autism Centre. (2021b, July 13). *Can children with autism pretend play?* Healis Autism Centre. https://www.healisautism.com/post/can-children-autism-pretend-play

Holland, K. (2021, November 1). *What you need to know about high-functioning autism.* Healthline.

https://www.healthline.com/health/high-
functioning-autism#support

*How to improve emotional self-regulation among children
with autism and attention disorders.* (2018,
December 3). Onlinegrad.pepperdine.edu.
https://onlinegrad.pepperdine.edu/blog/emotional-
self-regulation-children-autism/

Howard, A. (2021, November 23). *High-Functioning autism
symptoms (and controversy).* Psych Central.
https://psychcentral.com/autism/high-functioning-
autism-symptoms#about-high-functioning-autism

Hurley, K. (2022, February 2). *How to improve
communication with your ASD child.* Psycom.net -
Mental Health Treatment Resource since 1986.
https://www.psycom.net/autism-communication

Hutten, M. (n.d.-a). *Sensory stimulation for children on the
autism spectrum.* My ASD Child. Retrieved December
7, 2022, from
https://www.myaspergerschild.com/2008/08/provid
ing-sensory-stimulation-for-your.html

Hutten, M. (n.d.-b). *The telltale signs of high-functioning
autism: A comprehensive checklist.* My ASD Child.
Retrieved November 23, 2022, from
https://www.myaspergerschild.com/2017/11/the-
telltale-signs-of-high-functioning.html

Hutten, M. (n.d.-c). *Traits of High-Functioning Autism That Parents Should Be Aware Of*. My ASD Child. Retrieved November 23, 2022, from https://www.myaspergerschild.com/2018/08/traits-of-high-functioning-autism-that.html

Hutten, M. (2016, June). *Communication intervention and social skills training for kids on the spectrum*. My ASD Child. https://www.myaspergerschild.com/2016/06/communication-intervention-and-social.html

Hutten, M. (2021, May). *When your child with ASD does not "bond" well with you: Tips for moms*. My ASD Child. https://www.myaspergerschild.com/2021/05/when-your-child-with-asd-does-not-bond.html

Importance of play in developing social skills for children with autism. (2019, December 31). Nurture Pods Pte Ltd. https://www.nurturepods.com/importance-of-play-in-developing-social-skills-for-children-with-autism/

Integrity Inc admin. (2019, October 8). *Signs and symptoms of high functioning autism*. Integrity Inc. https://www.integrityinc.org/signs-and-symptoms-of-high-functioning-autism/

Integrity Inc. (2020, October 13). *Autism: Myths and misconceptions*. Integrity Inc.

https://www.integrityinc.org/autism-myths-and-

misconceptions/

*Interacting with a child who has autism spectrum disorder -

health encyclopedia - university of rochester medical

center.* (n.d.). Www.urmc.rochester.edu.

https://www.urmc.rochester.edu/encyclopedia/conte

nt.aspx?contenttypeid=160&contentid=46#:~:text=C

hildren%20with%20ASD%20respond%20best

Jurgens, A. (2017, October). *Communication: Children with

autism spectrum disorder.* Raising Children Network.

https://raisingchildren.net.au/autism/communicatin

g-relationships/communicating/communication-asd

Jurgens, A. (2021, May 19). *Communication: Autistic children.*

Raising Children Network.

https://raisingchildren.net.au/autism/communicatin

g-relationships/communicating/communication-

asd#:~:text=Communication%20skills%20are%20im

portant%20for

Kabr, S. (n.d.). *High-Functioning autism explained.* The Brain

Possible. Retrieved December 6, 2022, from

https://www.thebrainpossible.com/blog/high-

functioning-autism-explained

Lantz, J. (n.d.). *Play time: An examination of play

intervention strategies for children with autism

spectrum disorders: Articles: Indiana resource*

center for autism: Indiana university bloomington.

Indiana Resource Center for Autism.

https://www.iidc.indiana.edu/irca/articles/play-

time-an-examination-of-play-intervention-strategies-

for-children-with-autism-spectrum-disorders.html

Leafwing Centre. (2021, October 25). *Autism communication strategies*. LeafWing Center.

https://leafwingcenter.org/autism-communication-

strategies/

Lee, J., & Porretta, D. L. (2013). Enhancing the motor skills of children with autism spectrum disorders: A pool-based approach. *Journal of Physical Education, Recreation & Dance, 84*(1), 41–45.

https://doi.org/10.1080/07303084.2013.746154

Lesser, C. (2018, April 25). *How art therapy is helping children with autism express themselves*. Artsy.

https://www.artsy.net/article/artsy-editorial-art-

therapy-helping-children-autism-express

Lofland, K. B. (2013). *Helping your child to develop communication skills: Articles: Indiana resource center for autism: Indiana university bloomington.* Indiana Resource Center for Autism.

https://www.iidc.indiana.edu/irca/articles/helping-

your-child-develop-communication-skills.html

Loftus, Y. (2021a, February 23). *Communication problems and children with autism*. Autism Parenting Magazine. https://www.autismparentingmagazine.com/autism-children-communication-problems/

Loftus, Y. (2021b, June 7). *Autism strengths: Harnessing your child's abilities*. Autism Parenting Magazine. https://www.autismparentingmagazine.com/autism-strengths/

Lovering, N. (2022, May 3). *7 tips for parenting a child with "high functioning" autism*. Psych Central. https://psychcentral.com/autism/tips-for-parents-of-high-functioning-autistic-children#parenting-tips

Lowry, L. (2016). *Talking to young children on the autism spectrum matters, study shows*. Www.hanen.org. http://www.hanen.org/Helpful-Info/Articles/Talking-to-Young-Children-on-the-Autism-Spectrum.aspx

Lux AI Admin. (2021, July 29). *How to help children with autism handle their emotions; tips on supporting emotional regulation*. LuxAI S.A. https://luxai.com/blog/emotional-regulation-calm-down-activities-for-autistic-children/#practice-problem-solving-skills

Martino, R. (2015, July 21). *7 ways to increase social skills in children with autism*. Integrity Inc.

https://www.integrityinc.org/7-ways-to-increase-social-skills-in-children-with-autism/#:~:text=To%20promote%20socialization%20in%20children

Mason, S. A. (2013). Social stories. *Encyclopedia of Autism Spectrum Disorders*, 2935–2938. https://doi.org/10.1007/978-1-4419-1698-3_170

Matthews, A. (n.d.). *How to build a strong bond with your autistic child*. Parentinfluence.com. Retrieved December 6, 2022, from https://parentinfluence.com/how-to-build-a-strong-bond-with-your-autistic-child/

Mcilroy, A. T. (2021, August 13). *10 benefits of sensory play in early childhood*. Empowered Parents. https://empoweredparents.co/benefits-of-sensory-play/

McMillan, J. (2021, January 13). *Why autistics organize or line things up*. Thrive with Autism. https://thrivewithautism.ca/2013/09/06/why-autistics-organize-or-line-things-up/

McPherson, D. (2022, September 5). *Autism emotions: Recognizing and supporting your child's feelings*. Autism Parenting Magazine. https://www.autismparentingmagazine.com/recognizing-autism-emotions/

Melissa. (2020, July 2). *Teaching sorting skills in the classroom» autism adventures*. Autism Adventures. https://www.autismadventures.com/teaching-sorting-skills-in-the-classroom/

Mercado, E., Chow, K., Church, B. A., & Lopata, C. (2020). Perceptual category learning in autism spectrum disorder: Truth and consequences. *Neuroscience & Biobehavioral Reviews, 118*, 689–703. https://doi.org/10.1016/j.neubiorev.2020.08.016

Merriam-Webster. (2022). *Merriam-Webster dictionary*. Merriam-Webster.com; Merriam-Webster. https://www.merriam-webster.com/

Mezefsky, C. (2018, February 7). *Emotional Regulation in ASD*. Autism Research Institute. https://www.autism.org/webinars/emotional-regulation-in-asd/

Mohd Nordin, A., Ismail, J., & Kamal Nor, N. (2021). Motor development in children with autism spectrum disorder. *Frontiers in Pediatrics, 9*(15). https://doi.org/10.3389/fped.2021.598276

Myths and truth of high functioning autism spectrum. (2011). Www.theneurotypical.com. https://www.theneurotypical.com/myths-and-truths.html

National Institute on Deafness and Other Communication

Disorders. (2018, August 30). *Autism spectrum

disorder: Communication problems in children.*

NIDCD. https://www.nidcd.nih.gov/health/autism-

spectrum-disorder-communication-problems-

children

Nelson, H. D. (2018, September 6). *6 tips for interacting

positively with children on the autism spectrum.*

Intermountainhealthcare.org.

https://intermountainhealthcare.org/blogs/topics/pe

diatrics/2018/09/6-tips-for-interacting-positively-

with-children-on-the-autism-spectrum/

Nidirect. (2018). *How play helps children's development.*

Nidirect. https://www.nidirect.gov.uk/articles/how-

play-helps-childrens-development

Niedospial, L. (2020, August 10). *Why do toddlers almost

obsessively organize?* POPSUGAR Family.

https://www.popsugar.com/family/Why-Toddlers-

Organize-Line-Up-Toys-

44060675#:~:text=%22Organizing%20and%20sortin

g%20are%20important

Omahen, E. (2020, March 4). *Easy ways to help your child

with self-regulation.* Autism Parenting Magazine.

https://www.autismparentingmagazine.com/easy-

ways-with-self-regulation/

One Central Health. (2020, October 30). *10 myths about autism spectrum disorder*. One Central Health. https://www.onecentralhealth.com.au/autism/10-myths-about-autism/

Pal, S. (2014, August 29). *Early focus on gross motor skills may benefit children with autism | lower extremity review magazine*. Lermagazine.com. https://lermagazine.com/special-section/pediatric-clinical-news/early-focus-on-gross-motor-skills-may-benefit-children-with-autism

Patti. (2019, January 8). *The importance of sorting for children in a special education classroom*. Especiallyeducation.com. https://especiallyeducation.com/sorting-why-children-need-this-skill/#:~:text=Recognize%20and%20create%20patterns

Pietrangelo, A. (2021, September 13). *What is stimming and how can it be managed?* Healthline. https://www.healthline.com/health/autism/stimming#stimming-with-autism

Pietro, S. (2016, February 24). *Autism and stimming*. Child Mind Institute; Child Mind Institute. https://childmind.org/article/autism-and-stimming/

Play Learning Scholars Around the World | May 2020. (2020,

May 18). *Emotions expressed during play are

opportunities for learning through play.* Child and

Family Blog.

https://childandfamilyblog.com/learning-through-

play/

Quincy. (2020, June 17). *Autistic play is appropriate play.*

Speaking of Autism...

https://speakingofautismcom.wordpress.com/2020/

06/17/autistic-play-is-appropriate-play/

Rain, E. (2016, August 22). *10 gross motor activities for

autistic children.* Learning and Behavioral Center.

https://www.learningandbehavioralcenter.com/beha

vior-therapy-blog/10-gross-motor-activities-for-

autistic-children/

Remington, A. (2015, August 18). *Autistic people are more

creative than you might think.* The Conversation.

https://theconversation.com/autistic-people-are-

more-creative-than-you-might-think-46107

Richdale, A., & Green, C. (2017, June). *Sensory sensitivities:

Children and teenagers with autism spectrum

disorder.* Raising Children Network.

https://raisingchildren.net.au/autism/behaviour/und

erstanding-behaviour/sensory-sensitivities-asd

Richdale, A., & Green, C. (2020, November 19). *Obsessive behaviour, routines and rituals: Autistic children and teenagers*. Raising Children Network. https://raisingchildren.net.au/autism/behaviour/understanding-behaviour/obsessive-behaviour-asd#:~:text=And%20some%20autistic%20children%20have

Richdale, A., & Green, C. (2022, August 25). *Stimming: Autistic children and teenagers*. Raising Children Network. https://raisingchildren.net.au/autism/behaviour/common-concerns/stimming-asd#:~:text=Stimming%20is%20repetitive%20or%20unusual

Ropar, D., & Peebles, D. (2006). Sorting preference in children with autism: The dominance of concrete features. *Journal of Autism and Developmental Disorders, 37*(2), 270–280. https://doi.org/10.1007/s10803-006-0166-2

Rosenlund, J. (2021, April 29). *6 tips for communicating with children with autism*. Active Speech Pathology. https://www.activespeechpathology.com.au/blog/2021/4/29/6-tips-for-communicating-with-children-with-autism/

Roybal, B. (2020, December 4). *High-Functioning autism: What is it and how is it diagnosed?* WebMD. https://www.webmd.com/brain/autism/high-functioning-autism#:~:text=What%20is%20High%2DFunctioning%20Autism%3F&text=%E2%80%9CHigh%2Dfunctioning%20autism%E2%80%9D%20isn

Rudy, L. J. (n.d.). *8 ways to build a strong, loving bond with your autistic child.* Exceptional Family Center. Retrieved December 6, 2022, from https://www.kernefc.org/8-ways-to-build-a-strong-loving-bond-with-your-autistic-child.html

Rudy, L. J. (2022a, January 8). *Reasons why symptoms of high-functioning autism can be overlooked.* Verywell Health. https://www.verywellhealth.com/high-functioning-autism-260305

Rudy, L. J. (2022b, April 15). *How Can Play Therapy Benefit Your Child With Autism?* Verywell Health. https://www.verywellhealth.com/play-therapy-and-autism-the-basics-260059

Rudy, L. J. (2022c, May 7). *20 ways to help a child with autism to stay calm or manage meltdowns.* Verywell Health. https://www.verywellhealth.com/how-to-calm-a-child-with-autism-4177696

Rudy, L. J. (2022d, May 15). *Why autistic children play
differently*. Verywell Health.
https://www.verywellhealth.com/autistic-child-form-
of-play-
259884#:~:text=Children%20with%20autism%20pla
y%20differently%20than%20those%20who%20don

Rudy, L. J. (2022e, October 16). *Why do autistic children stim?*
Verywell Health.
https://www.verywellhealth.com/what-is-stimming-
in-autism-
260034#:~:text=Stims%20are%20behaviors%20like
%20rocking

Rutgers, A. H., van IJzendoorn, M. H., Bakermans-
Kranenburg, M. J., Swinkels, S. H. N., van Daalen, E.,
Dietz, C., Naber, F. B. A., Buitelaar, J. K., & van
Engeland, H. (2007). Autism, attachment and
parenting: A comparison of children with autism
spectrum disorder, mental retardation, language
disorder, and non-clinical children. *Journal of
Abnormal Child Psychology, 35*(5), 859–870.
https://doi.org/10.1007/s10802-007-9139-y

Sakellariou, A. (2022, June 1). *The proven benefits of sensory
play for toddlers*. BabyGaga.
https://www.babygaga.com/sensory-play-toddlers-
benefits/

Salus health - autism and communication problems. (2017).

    Www.salusuhealth.com.

    https://www.salusuhealth.com/Speech-Language-

    Institute/News/News-Stories/Autism-and-

    Communication-Problems.aspx

Sensory differences. (n.d.). Autism Tasmania.

    https://www.autismtas.org.au/about-autism/key-

    areas-of-difference/sensory-

    differences/#:~:text=Due%20to%20sensory%20sensi

    tivities%2C%20someone

Shafer, L. (2018, June 12). *Summertime, playtime*. Harvard

    Graduate School of Education.

    https://www.gse.harvard.edu/news/uk/18/06/summ

    ertime-playtime

Smith, L. (2022, March 16). *Stimming: Understanding this

    symptom of autism*. Www.medicalnewstoday.com.

    https://www.medicalnewstoday.com/articles/319714

    #complications

Smith, M., Segal, J., & Hutman, T. (2019, March 20). *Helping

    your child with autism thrive*. HelpGuide.org.

    https://www.helpguide.org/articles/autism-learning-

    disabilities/helping-your-child-with-autism-

    thrive.htm

Social skills for autistic children. (2021, May 19). Raising

    Children Network.

https://raisingchildren.net.au/autism/communicatin
g-relationships/connecting/social-skills-for-children-
with-asd#social-skills-what-they-are-and-why-theyre-
important-nav-title

Staff, E. (2020, January 8). *5 common myths about high
functioning autism*. Emerge Professionals.
https://emergeprofessionals.com/myths-high-
functioning-autism/

Study.com. (2021). *Teaching pretend play to children with
autism | study.com*. Study.com.
https://study.com/academy/lesson/teaching-
pretend-play-to-children-with-autism.html

Talton, L. (2021, September 3). *Five social skills activities for
children with autism*. Autism Parenting Magazine.
https://www.autismparentingmagazine.com/five-
social-skills-activities/

Team Stamurai. (2021, September 22). *8 speech therapy
exercises for children with autism*. Stamurai.com.
https://stamurai.com/blog/speech-therapy-exercises-
for-children-with-autism/

The Australian Parenting Website. (2017, August 2). *Social
skills for children with autism spectrum disorder*.
Raising Children Network.
https://raisingchildren.net.au/autism/communicatin

g-relationships/connecting/social-skills-for-children-

with-asd

The Lane Agency. (2016, March 23). *Play*. Scottish Autism.

https://www.scottishautism.org/services-

support/support-families/information-resources/play

Tips to help an autistic child develop social skills | NIDO®.

(n.d.). Www.nidolove.com. Retrieved December 6,

2022, from https://www.nidolove.com/tips-help-

autistic-child-develop-social-skills

Torrado, J. C., Gomez, J., & Montoro, G. (2017). Emotional

self-regulation of individuals with autism spectrum

disorders: Smartwatches for monitoring and

interaction. *Sensors, 17*(6), 1359.

https://doi.org/10.3390/s17061359

Tuchel, T. (2021, May 12). *Self regulation of emotions in

autism: 5 ways to help!* Autism Little Learners.

https://autismlittlelearners.com/self-regulation-of-

emotions/

Types of sensory issues in autism | behavioral innovations.

(2021, September 7). Behavioral Innovations - ABA

Therapy for Kids with Autism. https://behavioral-

innovations.com/blog/types-of-sensory-issues-in-

autism-examples-and-treatment-options/

Ure, A. (2022, April 28). *Recognising, understanding and

managing emotions: Autistic children and teenagers*.

Raising Children Network.

https://raisingchildren.net.au/autism/development/social-emotional-development/recognising-understanding-emotions-autistic-children-teens

Vance, T. (2022, August 4). *How to bond with your autistic child through your special interests*. NeuroClastic. https://neuroclastic.com/how-to-bond-with-your-autistic-child-through-your-special-interests/

Velentza, F. (2022, February 17). *The importance of play activities for children with autism*. Upbility Publications. https://upbility.net/blogs/news/the-importance-of-play-activities-for-children-with-autism

WebMD Editorial Contributors. (2021, April 21). *What you need to know about stimming and autism*. WebMD. https://www.webmd.com/brain/autism/what-you-need-to-know-about-stimming-and-autism

Weisstuch, Z. S. (2021, October 1). *The importance of socialization for individuals with autism spectrum disorders*. Autism Spectrum News. https://autismspectrumnews.org/the-importance-of-socialization-for-individuals-with-autism-spectrum-disorders/

Wieder, S. (2018, April 18). *DIR floortime & play therapy training | autism resources*. DIR Floortime & Play

Therapy Training | Autism Resources.

    https://profectum.org/motor-development-autism-

    affects-motor-skills/

Wise, J. (2022, January 19). *What are the benefits of exercise*

    for children with autism? – reach educational

    services. Reach Educational Services.

    https://reacheducationalservices.com/exercise-for-

    autistic-

    children/?utm_source=rss&utm_medium=rss&utm_

    campaign=exercise-for-autistic-children

Yeager, A. (2014, March 28). *Autism and motor skills: Benefits*

    of movement. TulsaKids Magazine.

    https://www.tulsakids.com/ways-movement-

    benefits-autistic-children/

Young, N. (2021, July 20). *Why creativity is so important for*

    children with autism. Geek Alabama.

    https://geekalabama.com/2021/07/19/why-

    creativity-is-so-important-for-children-with-autism/

9 798223 639992